WE CAN HAVE
BETTER
MARRIAGES

"I began to realise that . . . I would have to go to the heart of the family—the couple. They are the key to the love-revolution the world needs. . . . In many families I could see a characteristic, something special they had which was lacking in other families. I tried to discern what these special qualities were, and I concluded in time that the unique quality was the confidence and trust these couples had in each other."

Father Gabriel Calvo
founder of the Marriage Encounter movement*

*Father Gabriel Calvo, quoted by Antoinette Bosco in *Marriage Magazine,* June, 1973, p. 16.

WE CAN HAVE
BETTER
MARRIAGES
IF WE REALLY WANT THEM

by
David & Vera Mace

Nashville · ABINGDON

WE CAN HAVE BETTER MARRIAGES

Library of Congress Cataloging in Publication Data

MACE, DAVID ROBERT
 We can have better marriages if we really want them.
 Bibliography: p
  1. Marriage. 2. Interpersonal relations.
I. Mace, Vera, joint author. II. Title.
HQ728.M23   301.42   73-17468

ISBN 0-687-44282-6

MANUFACTURED BY THE PARTHENON PRESS AT
NASHVILLE, TENNESSEE, UNITED STATES OF AMERICA

*To the hundreds of couples
who have shared with us the discovery
that our marriages could be enriched
beyond all our expectations.*

*And to the millions of couples
who have yet to make
this exciting discovery.*

Preface

We are a couple now in our fortieth year of marriage. We are unanimously (two votes) of the opinion that marriage can be the most satisfying experience, or range of experiences, that human life has to offer. Each of us holds (individual votes) that the most significant and rewarding decision he or she has ever taken was to marry the other—"the best thing I ever did in my life," as Winston Churchill is reported to have said of his marriage.

Our marriage has grown and changed a great deal through the years. Like all couples, we have had our ups and downs. But we have never felt that marriage thwarted us as individuals, curtailed our freedom, or blocked our personal development or fulfillment. On the contrary, each of us has been able to make new ventures which have been possible only through the support of the other. Our individual lives have not been narrowed but broadened by our involvement in our shared corporate life. We offer this testimony because a contrary view of marriage is being loudly proclaimed today.

Early in our life together we reached the decision to devote the rest of our lives to the promotion of better marriages— our own and those of others who needed help. We both prepared for this through appropriate graduate studies and shaped our professional goals accordingly. In the course of time this led us into extensive travels, and involved us in programs and projects in our chosen field in sixty countries, with frequent return visits to many of them. These travels also brought us large numbers of cherished friends all over the world. We are profoundly thankful for these experiences and consider ourselves very fortunate people.

Now senior citizens, we look out upon the contemporary marriage scene and are somewhat disquieted. Not, we hasten to say, because we share the prevailing pessimism about marriage. Our concern is because, after a lifetime of studying the marriage relationship, both through books and in living specimens, we are convinced that the number of happy, successful marriages could be greatly increased, if only we could deal with widespread ignorance and stubborn indifference. There was a time when marriage was very poorly understood, and all that we could offer disappointed couples was superficial platitudes. We are not saying that today the mysteries of marital interaction are now an open book. But we *are* saying that we have made considerable progress in our understanding of this basic human relationship and that unfortunately we are not putting our new knowledge to very effective use.

This we consider to be a serious matter because we view the marriage relationship as being both the prototype of and the model for other adult human relationships. As marriage goes, so goes the family: as the family goes, so goes the community—this is not a cause and effect sequence of universal application, but we know of no other that remotely approaches it as a determinant of the quality of human society. When we are dealing with marriages, we are working deep down among the foundation stones of the entire cultural structure of mankind. So we believe; and although we claim to have open minds, nothing we have heard or read has yet convinced us to the contrary.

In recent years we have become involved in new approaches which are beginning to be identified by the term "marriage enrichment." In this movement we see great hope for the future. It is based on the assertion that marriage is a dynamic, and not a static, entity. The static concept no doubt derived from the legal emphasis on the contract and from the religious emphasis on the *stability* of marriage. It is a concept which has emphasized the *institution* and denied the central importance of the *relationship*. Such an emphasis may have served a useful purpose in the past; but it is neither relevant nor applicable to the hopes and expectations of married couples today.

We need therefore to see marriage in new terms, as a continually growing, continually changing, interaction between a man and a woman who are seeking the warmth and richness of the shared life. Marriage has too often been portrayed as two people frozen together side by side, as immobile as marble statues. More accurately, it is the intricate and graceful cooperation of two dancers who through long practice have learned to match each other's movements and moods in response to the music of the spheres.

We believe that by appropriate processes of marriage enrichment, which we have described and discussed in this book, multitudes of couples can find together the deeper joys, the richer fulfillment, and the fuller creativity which have until now seemed to mock them by holding out promises that could not be fulfilled. This is no miracle—it is simply the discovery and the patient, resolute cultivation of the potential for a loving relationship that is part of our human endowment.

We have divided our book into three parts, following a logical sequence. We begin with a review of modern marriage as it is being seen today from the outside, as a social unit. Next we adopt a different stance and view it, as an interpersonal relationship, from within. This dual approach allows us to develop our conviction that, both for the good of society and for the good of the individual, we need to help married couples promote the growth and enrichment of their relationship.

In the third part of the book we discuss in practical terms

some of the ways in which marriage enrichment can be promoted, drawing freely on our own experience and on the experiences of others, and venture to offer a practical proposal for the much greater involvement of married couples themselves in the promotion of extensive programs for marriage enrichment. In this exciting possibility we see the greatest hope of all for the future of marriage.

We have chosen to write our book in a particular manner. Covering such a broad subject, and with no lack of material, it could have grown into a very large volume. But this would have defeated our primary purpose. We believe we have some important things to say, and we hope the book will be widely read. We reasoned that we should therefore keep our chapters brief, saying what we had to say without "padding" each particular subject and then moving on quickly. For the same reason we have reduced documented references, which we could have provided in abundance, to a minimum.

We are grateful to a host of teachers, colleagues, and married couples who have shared their insights and experiences with us. We wish particularly to mention Clark Vincent, Director of the Behavioral Sciences Center where we work, whose concept of marital health, elaborated in his recent book,[1] has helped us to clarify and validate many of our own ideas. We are grateful also to Lucy Crawford and Eleanor Hill, who between them converted our rough manuscript into tidy typescript.

David and Vera Mace

---

[1] Clark E. Vincent, *Sexual and Marital Health* (New York: McGraw-Hill, 1973), p. 3.

Contents

PART I

Marriage Viewed from the Outside

CHAPTER 1

Marriage Under Attack

This is a book on how *good* marriage can be. We want to begin, however, by considering the views of a few of our contemporaries on how *bad* it can be.

Here is one of them:

Our expectations of marriage have transformed it into a ghetto of lunacy where two people put their antic dispositions on to play out roles of their, and society's, devising. In the attempt at impossible union, so much indignation, individuality, egoism and pride must be compromised that, finally, the separate personality laid on the Procrustean bed is fitted to an arbitrary slot. To be married means, too often, a capitulation to sameness, an end to self-development, and unnatural death of spirit. . . . It means the end of friendships that require sacrifice, and the end of risks. It leads to self-pity and overconsumption, to a conservatism that is moral and emotional as well as political and social. After a time, it brings out crazy fears of abandonment, of not being able to cope, of change, of desertion by children, of insufficiency. It causes the premature deaths of mind and soul through sexual rot and ploys for power. The expectations of marriage, dreamy and filmy, become a web to imprison the self.[1]

These words are taken from the opening paragraph of a recent book with the colorful title *Marriage Is Hell*. There is

[1] Kathrin Perutz, *Marriage Is Hell* (New York: William Morrow & Co., 1973), pp. 3-4.

plenty more in the same vein. The tirade against marriage is maintained, without slackening in intensity, throughout most of the book.

No doubt there are those who will recognize in these words an accurate portrayal of their marriages, past or present. With our background of many years' experience of marriage counseling, we are well aware that the estate of matrimony can indeed sink as low as that. But the author is not describing isolated cases of pathological degeneration. The implication is clearly that this is a description of contemporary marriages in general.

Since we are now in our fortieth year of a contemporary marriage, we have to protest that we simply do not recognize our relationship in this discouraging description. Indeed, a careful analysis of the statement would lead us to evaluate it as the precise opposite of what marriage has meant to us; and we would be entirely willing to submit ourselves to objective evaluation to prove the point. We could also, if necessary, furnish the names of a very large number of couples of our acquaintance who, we are certain, would share our evaluation. And beyond the circle of our immediate acquaintance, we are equally convinced, are millions more.

Who, it may then be asked, is the author of this pronouncement, asserted with such confident authority? According to the internal evidence provided by the book, she is a young woman still in her thirties, who suffered an unhappy adolescence during which she "often thought of suicide and nihilism." She also volunteers the information that she has a three-year-old son and has had three abortions; and, oddly enough, she is herself married, despite all her denunciations. Apart from a little exploration in history and anthropology to collect some useful references to support her point of view, there is no evidence that she is familiar with the authorities on contemporary marriage, or with the extensive researches carried out by scholars in the field.

We select Kathrin Perutz simply as a convenient illustration of what is happening on a wide scale. Since books attacking marriage and the family are in vogue today, an alert publisher may naturally decide to add one to his list. He approaches a talented young woman writer, apparently unconcerned about her lack of qualifications in the field. She agrees to take on the job.

With unusual candor, she describes in her preface what happened next. "I began reading at random on the subject of marriage and within a few weeks had filled a notebook with questions and arguments. I saw the possibilities of a theme; marriage as we know it is an anachronism in every way, but isn't recognized as such, and so the ground between expectations and reality is littered with dead hopes, unnecessary pain and wasted energies." [2] Thus, with the knowledge amassed by her few weeks of random reading, she launches into a series of pronouncements by way of enlightening the public about a human institution older than civilization.

Kathrin Perutz represents only the harassing snipers in the attack on marriage. Bigger salvos emerge from the heavy artillery. David Cooper in *The Death of the Family*[3] and Kate Millett in *Sexual Politics*[4] go so far as to suggest that the family has been the greatest disaster that ever happened to mankind and the cause of most of our woes.

Nor is this attack a recent phenomenon. George Bernard Shaw, the British playwright, in the preface to his play *Getting Married* wrote in 1908, "I could fill a hundred pages with the tale of our imbecilities and still leave much untold; but what I have set down here haphazard is enough to condemn the system that produced us. The cornerstone of that system was the family and the institution of marriage as we have it today

[2] *Ibid.* p. vii.
[3] David Cooper, *The Death of the Family* (New York: Pantheon Books, 1970).
[4] Kate Millett, *Sexual Politics* (Garden City, N.Y.: Doubleday, 1970).

in England." [5] Thomas Mann, the German novelist, wrote in 1926, "Truly one may, even without malice, easily gather the impression that today ninety percent of all marriages are unhappy." [6] Dr. Norman Haire, a radical physician and sex reformer of the same period, wrote, "Any moderately intelligent person who goes about the world with his eyes open —who is willing to face the truths of life even if they are disagreeable—must be struck by the appalling frequency of unhappiness in marriage. I can find no reason to believe that my circle of friends and acquaintances is an exceptional one, and if I am to judge by them I must conclude that a large majority of marriages are unsuccessful. . . . Speaking broadly, I should say that only one marriage in four may be judged as even tolerably successful, and a very much smaller proportion can fairly be considered as really happy." [7]

What is happening today is that the attack on marriage has become a form of public entertainment that suits the iconoclastic mood of our time, when extremists command attention and ridiculing the traditional institutions is a popular new sport. Examples abound. A newspaper columnist titles one of his discussions "The Marriage Mess." A woman attorney is announced as the speaker at a conference—her subject, "Is Marriage Lunacy?" A distinguished professional in the field is quoted in the *New York Times* magazine as saying sadly—"We know that somehow marriage stinks." [8]

A more ambitious effort was the January 26, 1971, issue of *Look,* which was given over to a discussion of the question —"Is The Family Obsolete?" Articles of varying length purported to give a representative sampling of reliable opinions. They included child specialists Benjamin Spock and Urie

[5] George Bernard Shaw, *Prefaces* (London: Constable, 1934), p. 7.
[6] Thomas Mann in H. Keyserling, ed., *The Book of Marriage* (New York: Harcourt and Brace, 1926), p. 258.
[7] Norman Haire, *Hymen: The Future of Marriage* (London: Kegan Paul, 1927), pp. 8 ff.
[8] Martha Weinman Lear, *The New York Times,* Aug. 13, 1972, p. 12.

Bronfenbrenner and anthropologist Margaret Mead; apart from these, they confined themselves to an actress, a classics professor, a college president, a feminist, and a social analyst. Other articles written by editorial staff leaned heavily on best-selling authors Kate Millett and Charles Reich, with a passing reference to William Goode, the only front-rank family sociologist whose views appeared to have been given any consideration. Ample space was of course lavished on cohabiting heterosexuals and homosexuals, to hippie experiments in communal living, and to the women's lib philosophy. The total result was an unbalanced assessment of a serious and important subject. We wrote a letter of protest to the editor, but to the best of our knowledge it was never printed.

We have already hinted at some of the possible motivations behind these attacks on marriage. There is of course the bid for attention that is characteristic of those who make risqué statements of any kind. There is also the compelling need of the extremist to make propaganda for his particular cause. Norman Haire was an avowed hedonist, so his statement about his circle of acquaintance being unexceptional must be treated with some reserve. David Cooper is a dedicated Marxist who dreams of the time, after the world Communist revolution, when we shall all live happily in communes. Kate Millett is a brilliant advocate of women's liberation who finds in the admittedly exploited lot of the traditional wife a persuasive means of enrolling disgruntled married women beneath the banner of the cause to which she is committed.

As for the professional writers, novelists, and playwrights, we know that as a class they have been publicly indulged by being awarded a degree of freedom, both in their novels and plays, and in their bohemian living patterns, that has not in the past been considered appropriate for the rest of us. They, together with actors and artists, have traditionally lived unorthodox lives out on the fringes of conventional society.

Much therefore can be explained away. But it cannot be

19

denied that modern marriages *are* in trouble on a fairly large scale. Therefore anyone who wants to attack marriage as an empty sham, as a device for the enslavement of women, or as an obsolescent institution, can easily find plenty of ammunition. Statistics and case material are freely available— you can take your choice. Both sound very impressive and can be used to paint a very distorted picture of what is really happening.

It is a well-established fact that a great deal of negative talk comes in time to surround a subject with an atmosphere of gloom. This has all been carefully studied and documented in the annals of psychological warfare. Undermine your enemy's confidence in his country, and you induce in him a mood of skepticism and despair which cuts the nerve of effort.

Particularly susceptible to this kind of propaganda are the young and inexperienced—especially if they have a predisposing tendency to be in a rebellious mood. These vicious attacks on marriage cannot therefore be dismissed as harmless exercises in sensationalism. They have succeeded in inducing in sections of today's youth a violent and denunciatory mood about marriage which goes far beyond a balanced appraisal of the facts.

In this book we shall try to present modern marriage in a more accurate perspective. What we shall do in this first part is to identify the main arguments advanced against marriage today and see how sound they are. We consider these arguments to be threefold:

1. Marriage restricts the freedom of the individual to express himself and to find personal happiness.

2. The marriage-based nuclear family is a less effective social unit than some of the new alternative life-styles.

3. Marriage stands revealed as a means by which men have enslaved women and denied them true personhood.

These will be the subjects of discussion in our next three chapters.

CHAPTER 2

The Tie That Binds—Or Does It?

The picture of marriage presented by its attackers portrays a rigid, intractable institution that puts those who enter it into a straitjacket which crushes their personality growth. It is a trap into which unsuspecting young people are enticed by false and empty promises only to find themselves locked up in a dismal prison house. It offers love and then engenders hate. It promises the unfolding of the personality and actually stultifies personality growth. It holds out the hope of ecstatic happiness and delivers abject misery. The theme could be further elaborated; but this represents, we think, the essence of the argument, which is that marriage is intolerably restrictive.

That there have been, and are, marriages that result in all this misery we will readily concede. But that marriage is necessarily like this, or always like this, we must stoutly deny. Let us examine the matter more closely.

Freedom represents an ideal which has vital importance in our Western culture. But it was not always so. Human history has been, for the most part, a long, depressing record of exploitation. Ruthless tyrants, in a seemingly endless succession, have seized power and subjected whole peoples. Petty oppressors have imitated them at lower levels of the social structure. Slavery, in one form or another, has reduced men and women to chattels bought and sold in the marketplace. In feudal societies, peasants have been completely under the dominion of landowners. In early industrial communities, poorly paid workers have had to toil from dawn to dusk in what Blake called the "dark, Satanic mills."

It is little wonder, then, that we value our freedom. Millions in this century have fought and died to preserve it. American democracy represents the most advanced of the world's civilizations in terms of its dedication to the cause of individual liberty.

And so we are free, and we want to remain free. What however, does this mean? What is freedom for? And what sort of freedom do we really want? Strangely enough, this is a subject seldom discussed. We seem more ready to fight for freedom, and to extol it, than to sit down and examine just what it is all about in terms of our individual lives, and particularly in terms of our relationships with others.

There is, for example, an idea abroad that freedom means detachment from all involvement with others, all commitment to others, all duties and obligations, all social responsibilities. If this were really so, then humanity's model would be Robinson Crusoe on his desert island or the solitary hermit in his lonely cave.

This is certainly not what we want. The most dreaded of all forms of punishment is solitary confinement, which cuts one off entirely from all human communication. This is intolerable to us because we are social beings. We need and want involvement with others.

All right, we need involvement. But what kind of involvement? Is freedom the right to take from others without giving in return, to exploit others for our own benefit? To do this would be to return to tyranny, which means achieving our own freedom and independence at the expense of others.

So freedom must involve giving as well as taking. It is reciprocal action achieved in relationships based on mutual help and support, the sharing of joys and sorrows, and the willingness to sacrifice our own needs and goals, when the occasion requires it, in the interests of those to whom we are bound by ties of loyalty and affection. This kind of mutual interdependence is not confined to human beings; it is a pattern found widely throughout the animal kingdom as well.

Our interdependence is therefore based on the fact that we need each other. We need the help and cooperation of others in the tasks that are essential to our common safety and welfare. We need each other also for the exchange of thoughts and ideas, for comfort and reassurance in times of trouble, for fun and recreation, for training the next generation to take over and preserve our human culture.

We need not only involvement, but commitment. We need each other not simply for today, but also for tomorrow. We have to cooperate in getting this particular job done; but unless we can also count on cooperation in the next job, and the next, we have no security. If I have stood by you through this week's crisis, you want to be able to count on me if another crisis develops. This is what commitment means—an undertaking on my part that I am a dependable and trustworthy person, ready to enter into obligations and to meet them when the time comes. If I say I will pay you tomorrow and don't, if I promise to work with you till the job is done and then fail to show up, if I tell you I love you today and treat you with hostility and indifference next week—if I act in ways like these, I leave you confused and uncertain about what our relationship really means. Repeated acts of this kind by large numbers of people would finally break down the whole fabric of human society.

If therefore we interpret freedom as making it justifiable and right for us to confine involvement with others to what suits our individual interest and to refuse commitment except when it proves to be convenient, we are not building democracy, but tearing it down.

So far we have been discussing what our unwillingness to be involved and committed could do to others. Equally important is what it could do to ourselves. Involvement and commitment are not only the means by which human society functions, they are also the means by which human personality develops. Our concept of a mature person is not of one who asserts his own rights over against those of others, or "does his own thing" without regard for the consequences to others. A mature person is one who has learned to bring his self-esteem and his esteem for others into equilibrium—one who understands, accepts, and respects himself in such a way as to understand, accept, and respect others too. The goal of human life is not self-sufficiency, detachment, and indifference to others. It is positive and creative involvement with others, in relationships that exemplify love in the true meaning of that misunderstood and much abused word.

Because we are inextricably involved with others in mutual interdependence, the true art of living is to achieve the kind of relationships that are as loving as we are able to make them. As Havelock Ellis used to put it, "To live is to love and to love is to live." In other words, since we must relate to others because the self needs such involvement for its development and nourishment, self-fulfillment means making these relationships positive and constructive instead of negative and destructive.

If therefore we define freedom as a state of being largely uninvolved and uncommitted, we are denying ourselves relationships of any meaningful kind. To enter a relationship with the proviso that involvement must be limited in order that commitment may be avoided is like driving your car with the brake on in order to insure against a possible accident. The relationship is, by the very terms under which it is entered, deprived of the possibility of full development.

Let us now apply all this to marriage. Even if we aspire to be loving persons, in the nature of the case we can't love everybody. There are just too many people; and in the nature of the case they are not all congenial to us. So we build our relationships selectively and pick out a small group of people with whom it is possible to become involved in ways that are mutually helpful and supportive. This for some people brings all the satisfactions they need.

Most of us, however, seem to need in addition one in-depth relationship of greater involvement and of more lasting commitment. This need for a one-to-one relationship in which we give ourselves, and find ourselves, through total sharing with another seems to be a widespread and fundamental human need.

We think this need is connected with the ultimate validation of our selfhood. The foundation stone of all mental health is an assured confidence in our own worth as persons. We strive in many ways to achieve this assurance—by accumulating wealth, power, and status, for example. But always the nagging question remains: "Am I really esteemed for myself and for what I am, or for my money, my position, my achievements?" There is only one finally satisfying answer to that question. I cannot fully know myself, accept myself, and believe in myself until I am fully known, accepted, and truly and consistently loved by someone who totally shares my life. We believe that what people fundamentally seek in marriage is this convincing self-validation and that this is the ultimate *summum bonum* which a good marriage bestows on both partners.

We shall discuss further aspects of this need later in the book. But there is plenty of evidence that it exists and that those who are able to fulfill it become deeply contented persons. It is also true that many fail to fulfill it, suggesting that to do so is a complex and difficult task.

The human institution which we call marriage is obviously well designed to meet this need. It fulfills other purposes as well and has taken many forms. But it has been a very persistent, and to all intents universal, human institution. When viewed objectively, it is also a very ingenious arrangement.

A man and a woman come together in a shared life. They

set up a home together. They meet each other's sexual needs. They cooperate in providing the basic necessities for survival, and beyond that as many comforts and conveniences as possible. They talk and listen to each other. They comfort and support each other. They share thoughts and ideas, hopes and fears, joys and sorrows. They enjoy fun and recreation together. They establish rituals to celebrate the great occasions of human life. Within the wider community they create an inner private life of intimacy, of deep mutual involvement, of complete openness to each other. They raise children and together launch them into the future. In this way they provide a nuclear unit of human society, a medium through which the culture is maintained and passed on to the next generation.

If we had never heard of marriage and it was now being proposed to us for the first time, we would probably react by saying it was a wonderful idea. It meets so many fundamental needs and wraps up so many things that are important to humanity in one neat package that we would certainly want to establish it if this had not already been done.

In fact, it has been with us for a very long time. And what many people are proposing to us today is not that it should be established, but that it should be abolished! This seems a very strange idea. What has gone wrong?

What has happened is that the basic concept of marriage, encrusted with many accretions from our cultural past, has collided head on in a resounding clash with the most advanced concepts of individual freedom which have so far evolved. This was probably inevitable, and the encounter should lead in the end to good results because it will force us to reexamine both our concept of marriage and our concept of individual freedom. At the moment, however, a lot of heat is being generated, a good many sparks are flying, and unfortunately a number of people are getting hurt.

In the past, as we have seen, freedom has not always been a high priority, and it has often been abused and violated.

This has happened in government, in religion, in community life—and in marriage. To see how this came about, we must consider a few facts about marriage as it has existed in the past.

Since the family constituted the foundation stone of human society, it was at first considered a duty for everyone to marry. A man who failed to do so was regarded as an oddity, and he might even, as in Hebrew society, be challenged on his failure to take a wife. Women were likewise married off wherever possible, and no other respectable career was available to those who weren't. This undiscriminating demand that everyone should marry denied freedom of choice by recognizing no other acceptable option.

In many cultures young people were segregated by sex, so that they had no opportunity of meeting and getting to know each other. This was tied in with a system of "arranged" marriages. Instead of choosing marriage partners for themselves, boys and girls had to submit to choices made for them by their parents. Sometimes these turned out to be wise and good choices; but the point was that individuals were denied freedom to choose for themselves. This was of course true also, in large measure, of other basic choices, like that of a vocation. Today, however, we would regard any such limitation of choice as a violation of personal freedom.

Once a couple were married, they were normally expected to live either with the bridegroom's parents, or to be under the supervision of the parents on both sides. They had to endure considerable interference in the way they managed their private lives, often no doubt well intended, but nonetheless irritating. This was particularly frustrating to the wife who was often dominated by her mother-in-law and given little opportunity of expressing her own wishes. The assumption that the husband held the final power of decision in all matters intensified the humiliation of the wife. These arrangements involved many gross violations of individual freedom.

To make matters worse, it was very difficult, if not impossible, to get out of an intolerable marriage. Divorce was frowned upon or completely denied. The only solution was to suppress all feelings of unhappiness and unfulfillment and to endure the misery with as much fortitude as one could command.

So our traditional marriage institution can justly be attacked in the name of individual freedom. Clearly some radical changes need to be made. First, no one should be put under obligation to marry. Second, young people should have the right to choose freely the person they wish to marry. Third, married couples should be allowed to set up their own separate homes and should not be required to submit to their parents' management of their affairs. Fourth, the wife should have equal status with her husband in the partnership of marriage. Fifth, in the event of a marriage turning out to be completely unworkable, the possibility of choosing to terminate it by divorce should be available. These five points might constitute a charter for marriage, delivering it from the injustices of the past and bringing it into line with the principles of human freedom and independence. Until these conditions have been met, the advocates of true democracy have the right to keep up their demands.

But wait a minute! What are we talking about? People don't *have* to marry today. Young people *are* free to make their own choices. Married couples *do* set up their own independent homes. Wives *are* regarded as equal partners with their husbands. And divorce *is* available to those who can't make marriage work.

In other words, all the legitimate demands that could reasonably be made in the name of human freedom have already been met or are in the process of being met. Marriage has in fact undergone a major adaptation within the context of our democratic society. So who is complaining, and about what? What's the purpose of writing books to say marriage is restrictive? If that's the way it seems to you, then leave it alone; or, if you're already in it, get out of it! What's all the fuss about?

That's an important question. Why are the attacks on marriage, based on the concept of freedom, being stepped up when in fact all reasonable demands are already being met? We have given this question a good deal of thought and have tried to come up with an intelligible answer.

Who wants to attack marriage and why? And who wants to hear marriage attacked and why? Not persons who are married and satisfied, obviously. And presumably not persons who prefer the single life. It comes down, surely, to two groups of people—those who have tried marriage and found that it failed to meet their needs; and those who once looked upon marriage with high hopes and expectations but have now been persuaded that their dreams can't come true.

In other words, the disillusioned. Those who are frustrated by the belief that the promise held out to them cannot be fulfilled because they are doomed to endure the tortures of Tantalus, whose thirst could never be satisfied because the water of the lake in which he stood receded whenever he reached down to drink.

Come to think of it, there are a great many such people in American society today. There are the divorced, who went into marriage with the same hopes and dreams as the rest of us but in the end had to admit defeat. Most of them marry again in time; but there are eight million one-parent families in the United States today, and most of these parents have left a broken marriage behind them. There are also the young people who have seen, or believe they have seen, in the sterile marriages of their parents and elders something very different from the dream of romantic bliss that was sold to an earlier generation but will no longer be bought by the more enlightened youth of today.

Add all these together, and you have a positive vineyard of

sour grapes. To these people, striving to bury the aspirations which they now have little hope of fulfilling, what could be more fortifying than the assurance that marriage is a colossal fraud, a will o' the wisp, an entangling growth that hinders real personality development and frustrates true self-expression? And marriage can be just that for those who have known only superficial unions which never developed genuine sharing or relationship-in-depth. As we shall see later, the compulsive clutching at each other that is characteristic of insecure marriages is restrictive in the extreme. Only when two people know, trust, and love each other can they give each other complete freedom and support each other's growth to full autonomy.

Our theory that many who attack marriage are only trying to stifle their own inner feelings of frustration seems to be supported by the fact that many of the young cynics do marry in the end and most of the divorced remarry. Some of the angry outbursts against marriage seem to resemble the exasperation of the child who, after failing to win the game, vents his frustration on his playmates not only by refusing to play any more but also by trying to break up the game for others.

We may sum up by saying that the argument that marriage is a straitjacket remains, at the very least, not proven. The straitjacket may indeed be an apt description of a bad marriage, which of course is bad for all concerned. But in this book we are not attempting to defend bad marriage, which is indefensible anyway. We are concerned with promoting good marriages, and we are convinced that we could and should have more of them because we believe that a good marriage represents a proper and responsible use and fulfillment of individual freedom and provides an ideal setting for healthy personality development.

CHAPTER 3

Those Alternative Life-Styles

"There will of course always be large numbers of people who for some reason or other will not marry, who are not suitable for marriage, who never fall in love or cannot marry the one they fall in love with, who do not miss the kind of home provided by married life, who have no desire for children. Marriage is not made for everybody, not attractive to everybody, not good for everybody who embarks in it." [1]

These are the words of Edward Westermarck, one of the most distinguished of all students of human marriage. They appear in his book *The Future of Marriage in Western Civilization,* published nearly forty years ago.

What is interesting is that Westermarck refers to "large numbers" of people who don't marry. He was a Scandinavian by birth, who later settled in England; and he wrote in the 1930s. He was making a point that may surprise some Americans. The idea is widely held that in Europe forty years ago nearly everyone married, whereas today many are choosing to reject matrimony. In fact, the very opposite is true. Americans have always tended to marry in larger numbers than Northern Europeans; and the proportion of Americans marrying in our present era has been higher than ever before.

Despite these facts, there is a great deal of talk today about doing away with marriage and replacing it with some-

[1] Edward Westermarck, *The Future of Marriage in Western Civilization* (London: Macmillan, 1936), pp. 170-71.

thing else. A book has recently been published entitled *The Nuclear Family in Crisis: The Search for an Alternative.*[2] The implication would seem to be that we must find something to take the place of our present family system before it finally collapses. Again, this is not a new idea. George Bernard Shaw, writing in 1908, did not mince matters. He referred to the conventional family as "the Holy of Holies in the temple of honorable motherhood, innocent childhood, manly virtue, and sweet and wholesome national life. But with a clever turn of the hand this Holy of Holies can be exposed as an Augean stable, so filthy that it would seem more hopeful to burn it down than to attempt to sweep it out."[3]

The *nuclear* family, as it has been called, is easily distinguished as the group consisting of husband and wife and their growing children—the typical family unit of today. It is contrasted with the *extended* family—a larger unit which also includes other relatives. It can be extended vertically to include grandparents and grandchildren; or horizontally to include brothers or sisters and their families. It can also be extended in both directions, and include a variety of more distant relatives. In Malaysia we were once the guests of such a family, which included so many members that we failed to count them all; but at night we did count about forty pairs of shoes at the foot of the stairs leading up to the children's sleeping quarters!

A favorite argument against marriage today is that the nuclear family has proved unworkable and that we must go back to the extended family in some shape or form, for our own sakes and for our children's sakes. Let us examine that argument.

A number of very misleading statements have been made recently about the nuclear family, and we want to set the

[2] Michael Gordon, *The Nuclear Family in Crisis* (New York: Harper & Row, 1972).
[3] Shaw, *Prefaces,* pp. 26-27.

record straight. Widely respected authorities who should have known better (we shall refrain from exposing them publicly) have to our knowledge stated or written that the nuclear family was unknown before the Industrial Revolution when it replaced the extended family, which had been the standard pattern up to that point.

This is sheer nonsense. The nuclear family is the basic building block out of which the overwhelming majority of human families, comprising a wide variety of patterns (including extended families), are fashioned. Some authorities (Desmond Morris[4] among them) hold that our earliest human ancestors, the hominids, when they were forced down from the trees and took to hunting as a means of survival, established nuclear families and retained that pattern for nearly two million years until man developed agriculture. Even in agricultural societies, genuine extended families were the exception rather than the rule. In China, for instance, a study of old census returns[5] shows that the average family had only six to eight members; which suggests, since many children were customary, that most families were nuclear. We could provide further evidence, but we hope we have made our point.

In our travels abroad we have seen many extended families in action. They require rigid discipline to hold them together. This is achieved by a hierarchical balance of authority and power—older members over younger, men over women—which ensures order and disciplined cooperation. Despite strict discipline, however, they seldom achieve harmony, but are often hotbeds of petty jealousy, intrigue, and strife. When any serious attempt is made to democratize them, they fall apart in ruins and tend to regroup in the form of nuclear families. This is a process we have observed again and again.

[4] Desmond Morris, *The Naked Ape* (New York: McGraw-Hill, 1967).
[5] David and Vera Mace, *Marriage: East and West* (Garden City, N.Y.: Doubleday, 1959), pp. 34-35.

Yet extended families meet a deep human need—the need for the controls and the supports of broad kinship relationship, and the sense of continuity and security that results. The mobile nuclear family of today is suffering from the lack of these controls and supports. It is isolated from close links with other family groups and constellations. This makes it very fragile and very brittle, and may result in serious deprivation for the children of poorly functioning parents.

So the search is on for alternatives. Many are under consideration. We are concerned in this book only with heterosexual relationships, so we need not embark on a discussion of homosexual marriages, except to recognize the fact that they are taking place and that there is a movement to get them officially recognized.

The alternatives which involve heterosexual relationships seem to be based on the principle we have already discussed —that the traditional marriage bond is too tight, creating a stifling and stultifying confinement of the lives of the partners. The alternatives are all designed to remedy this supposedly grave defect, and four or five principal proposals are involved.

First, what is called "serial monogamy." The contention is that it is unreasonable for a man and woman to be expected to stay together for a lifetime, because after some years they will become utterly bored with each other. Therefore the right to change partners from time to time should be fully recognized. This is of course what already exists in our society. The American divorce rate being what it is, the average American already has a higher number of marriage partners in the course of a lifetime than the average man in some African countries that practice polygamy. However, those who champion serial monogamy are not satisfied with our present arrangements. They want full social recognition to be given to changes of partners, as an inherent right rather than, as at present, as a reluctant concession.

The second alternative is what Albert Ellis has called

"civilized adultery." [6] This calls for recognition of the view that a little sexual variety might brighten up a dull marriage and that what was once viewed as a violation of marriage should therefore now be recognized as an asset to it. The most prominent example of this new attitude is of course the mate-swapping cult. It is difficult to determine whether this should be considered a loose form of monogamy, or a mild form of polygamy. Perhaps it is not an alternative life-style at all, but a form of recreation.

The third proposal is to reintroduce the ancient custom of multiple marriage, which is still practiced, though on a diminishing scale, in some areas of the world. There are many variants of the polygamous revival, and the distinctions between them are not always clear. Anthropologists have traditionally categorized multiple marriages as polygyny (one husband with more than one wife) and polyandry (one wife with more than one husband), but new terms like "multilateral marriage" are now emerging, and it will take some time for the terminology to be standardized.

The fourth proposal is a system of "group marriage" such as is reported from some communes, where a number of people of both sexes live together in a shared life that provides them all, in principle at least, with sexual access to one another and common responsibility for all their children. The concept of group marriage has always featured in anthropological literature, and examples have been cited from various societies (including the ancient Britons, as reported by Julius Caesar). There has been controversy, however, about whether such arrangements, notoriously loose and unstable, could justifiably be described as a form of marriage at all.

A fifth life-style, though it cannot be in any sense ranked as a form of marriage, is the single life involving a series of

---

[6] Albert Ellis, *The Civilized Couples' Guide to Extramarital Adventure* (New York: Wyden, 1972).

episodes with any number of sexual partners with no commitment of any kind.

A great deal of publicity has been given to these alternative life-styles, and there is no need for us to discuss them in detail here. We do, however, want to make a few general comments.

It is interesting to notice that these new forms are not so much alternatives *to* marriage, as alternative forms *of* marriage. Throughout human history, marriage has existed in many variant patterns. Westermarck's original definition, coined in 1891, is still serviceable—"a relation of one or more men to one or more women which is recognized by custom or law and involves certain rights and duties both in the case of the parties entering the union and in the case of children born of it." [7]

According to this definition, all but the fifth life-style would count as forms of marriage. The first two, in fact, retain a monogamous base, and the nuclear family pattern, but permit either a periodical change of partners or indulgence in extramarital sex. They depart, that is to say, respectively from the principle of indissolubility (held doctrinally by Catholics) and from the principle of fidelity (held by Jews and Christians).

The third alternative style goes further and departs from the monogamous pattern. We may note in passing that reliable reports indicate that these polygamous experiments are proving to be highly unstable. This is not surprising to us. We are very familiar with polygamous African customs, and years ago an African expert summed them up neatly by describing polygamy as "inherently factious." Normally it can be maintained as a marriage system only under rigid cultural controls, and generally only in communities where women are kept in abject submission.

[7] Edward Westermarck, *The History of Human Marriage*, Volume I (London: Macmillan, 1925), p. 26.

Another point worthy of notice is that the polygamous forms are being experimented with almost exclusively by relatively young people, mainly in their twenties. After a period in a polygamous marriage arrangement of some sort, the participants appear to go their separate ways and, soon after, to "settle down" to monogamous marriage. On the basis of these ascertained facts, Carlfred Broderick and others suggest that what we are witnessing here is simply the typical experimental behavior of young people in the interim stage of development in which they have left their parental families but have not yet established families of their own. Havelock Ellis[8] long ago described the "polyerotic" phase of psychosexual development through which young people pass before arriving at the "monoerotic" phase in which they marry. Young men in Europe traditionally went through a recognized period of sexual adventuring (often referred to as "sowing their wild oats") before they took wives and accepted family responsibilities. What is new is that young women are now claiming the same privilege. However, complaints have been heard by some of these young women that the men are using these new experiments in living as a rich opportunity for sexual exploitation. Jessie Bernard has reported to us that this criticism has occurred again and again in her discussions with girls living in communes or other group arrangements.[9]

As we try to see these experiments in clear perspective, we cannot escape the conclusion that their importance has been greatly exaggerated. They have provided sensational material that must come close to a press reporter's dream—sexual escapades, defiance of conventions, extremism, novelty—and have been publicized accordingly. But when we objectively examine what is going on, we find little that is new. The periodic exchange of marriage partners has already become

[8] Havelock Ellis, *Psychology of Sex* (New York: Emerson Books, 1946), p. 282.
[9] Dr. Jessie Bernard in a personal communication.

an accepted aspect of the American way of life. Adultery has been widely practiced for a long time, as every student of social history and every experienced marriage counselor is well aware. All that has happened is that it is now more openly practiced. Sexual experimentation is as old as mankind, and all we are now witnessing is a new atmosphere of tolerance which makes it no longer necessary to hide behind an elaborate system of subterfuge. One result is that the number of persons participating in these freer forms of man-woman relationship is probably increasing—this is certainly true of women. These facts may have significant implications for our future.

The alternative life-styles will no doubt continue to be practiced, and it will be interesting to watch how they develop. As Carl Rogers points out in his perceptive book *Becoming Partners,*[10] those who take those experiments seriously may enable us to learn a great deal about interpersonal relationships. Some people will inevitably get hurt; other people will benefit. But statements to the effect that these new patterns of living show marriage to be a dying institution, about to be replaced by something new and radically different, are simply not supported by the known facts. Monogamous marriage and the nuclear family are very old and very durable institutions, which have shown remarkable flexibility in adapting to a great variety of human environments. They are furnishing evidence, in our contemporary culture, that they have by no means lost this adaptive capacity. In our opinion, the really significant changes likely to take place are not so much in the outward form of marriage, as in its interior structure. We shall examine this fully in Part II of our book.

[10] Carl Rogers, *Becoming Partners: Marriage and Its Alternatives* (New York: Delacorte, 1972).

CHAPTER 4

Does Marriage Discriminate Against Women?

What is really new in the attack on marriage is the savage nature of the denunciations that are coming from the leaders of some women's groups. Traditionally, marriage and motherhood have been viewed as the realms where woman reigns supreme, where she finds her personal fulfillment and makes her vital contribution to human progress. We are therefore startled to find her now fouling her own nest, renouncing her past glory, and toughly demanding a square deal.

The message, however, is quite clear. The whole theme of Kate Millet's book *Sexual Politics* is that men have seized the power and control throughout human society, denied woman's personhood, and relegated her to a position of subjection. By sentimentalizing her role as wife and mother, and putting her on a pedestal by a tongue in cheek show of chivalry, the man has put her in a state of sedation and kept her unaware of her abject state of subservience.

Others have echoed this accusation. "Marriage means rape and life-long slavery," [1] cries Ti-Grace Atkinson. "Women in this movement," declares Rosalind Loring, "believe that inevitably love has caused, and will continue to cause, their downfall. Second-class status, loss of identity, lack of autonomy . . . all are due to love. Love has been used as a tool both by men and institutions of society to keep women in

[1] Ti-Grace Atkinson, "The Oppressed Majority Demands Its Rights," *Life*, Dec. 12, 1969.

their place, and historically that place has been defined by men. The result has kept women from achieving their potential, from gaining ego strength, from being fully functioning human beings." [2] Robin Morgan says, "One thing does seem clearer as time goes on; the nuclear family unit is oppressive to women." [3] And Mary Daly makes the same point by quoting a psychoanalyst who says, "Therapy often reveals a woman who has the impression of nonexistence resulting from the annihilation of her personality identity by her duties as wife and mother." [4] These quotations are typical. They are of course only opinions. But they are supported by facts. Jessie Bernard, in her book *The Future of Marriage*,[5] has cited evidence to support the general conclusion that marriage today is on the whole better for men than for women and that life is now less satisfying for the married woman than for her unmarried sister. If this is so, clearly the matter must be realistically faced, by men and women alike.

Before this can be done, however, it is necessary to ask ourselves how we got into this situation. Did the system really develop out of a vast malicious conspiracy on the part of men to exploit women, as seems to be implied? Or did it emerge out of historical necessity? The implication that women in the past have been generally discontented with their lot, while men have been satisfied with theirs, can also be challenged.

In the thousands of years during which traditional marriage has been the accepted pattern, it has been only relatively recently—say in the past hundred and fifty years—that its rightness for human society, particularly for women, has been

[2] Rosalind Loring, "Love and Women's Liberation" in Herbert Otto, ed., *Love Today: A New Exploration* (New York: Association Press, 1972), pp. 73-74.

[3] Robin Morgan, *Sisterhood Is Powerful* (New York: Random House, 1970), p. xxxii.

[4] Mary Daly, *The Church and the Second Sex* (New York: Harper & Row, 1968), p. 32.

[5] Jessie Bernard, *The Future of Marriage* (New York: World Publishing Co., 1972), pp. 17-18, 27-28.

challenged. Previously, marriage was both the goal and the ideal of women in general. It was an ideal that was maintained by society and supported by its institutions, such as the church, the legal system, current literature and philosophies. To be accepted at all, a woman *had* to conform to the pattern by becoming a submissive wife and, in due course, if possible, a devoted mother to numerous children. In return for this conformity, which was in general given eagerly and willingly, the two great boons of marriage were conferred— status and support. The status might mean a complete absence of any love or even affection, in spite of romantic ideas and hopes; and the support might be very precarious. But these hardships were accepted with fortitude, because public mores and society's protocol stood squarely in support of the institution of marriage. For any woman to contemplate rejection of the pattern was almost unthinkable, and the alternatives were truly frightful. The few vigorously independent women who first dared even to question the pattern had to be willing to face ignominy, loss of the experience of woman's supreme fulfillment, the contemptuous humor of their peers, and above all, poverty which could be mitigated only by remaining at home with the status of despised poor relations or such humiliating employment as that of a governess. In 1804 Jane Austen made a character in one of her novels say, "I would rather be a teacher at a school (and I can think of nothing worse) than marry a man I did not like." [6]

Under these circumstances, did marriage discriminate against women? Judged by today's standards, the answer must obviously be yes. But judged by the standards of the last century, it could with equal vehemence be no.

What then makes the difference? The fact that modern women have options such as were nonexistent, and undreamed of, even a century ago. No girl *has* to marry today to achieve

[6] Jane Austen in an unfinished novel known as *The Watsons*, begun in 1804.

41

status. She may in fact choose to marry for this reason, among others; and many a modern girl still does. But sooner or later, she is likely to have to acknowledge that the only real status which modern marriage can bestow upon the wife is the opportunity to develop personhood in her own right within the marriage. If she had no desire for this before marriage and has no will to work for it after marriage, she cannot blame marriage for her misfortune. She must blame herself.

Can women win status as persons in modern marriage? We believe they can. But it is a new kind of status, and wives will not achieve it alone in isolation from their husbands. Its achievement means a revolution (a complete turning around) in the thinking and practice of both women and men in marriage. We see this as one of the fundamentals of marriage enrichment.

The other reason for which women were lured into marriage in the past was in order to gain economic security; and the more money the husband had the better the marriage was deemed to be. Becky Sharp, in Thackeray's *Vanity Fair,* unhesitatingly adopted every artifice in the attempt to induce the loathsome and contemptible Joseph Sedley to marry her —because he was rich. This concept of marriage is still widely held today. There are still many women who opt for the arrangement whereby, in return for adequate shelter, food, clothes, and sustenance, they will give their total, continuous, unpaid, and sometimes completely unrecognized services. In our judgment this kind of marriage discriminates against the women who embrace it, whether they would agree or not.

These two desirable goals—status and support—with which the marriage trap was baited for women did, and do, represent discrimination of a kind that must be denounced as intolerable. However, with regard to both of them, the situation is today greatly changed, and is continuing to change. Indeed, we discern in modern marriage a whole series of subtle but radical changes, which bid fair to end totally the possibility of discrimination in the not too distant future. By way of illustration, here are four of them:

1. No one need look very far today to find marriages in which women are carrying a full share in the financial support of the family. This implies much more than the temporary "PHT" (Putting Hubby Through) endeavors of student days. Wives who wanted to earn money independently have in the past been a great problem to their husbands, who saw this as a threat to their masculinity and a judgment on their ability to provide for their wives and children. One wife, who earned considerably more than her husband, described to us the annual trauma of preparing the income tax return.

Yet many couples are resolving this problem. It means that they have to develop together a new kind of cooperative marriage in which wife and husband establish mutuality at all levels, a marriage in which discrimination is impossible to sustain.

Without implying approval of what women are so far paid in a man's world, we suggest that the breakdown of discrimination in this area, within marriage, will inevitably help to break down the discrimination women suffer outside marriage.

2. The emancipation of women, both overtly and working at hidden levels, has taken great leaps forward during times of war, national crisis, and major cultural change. Why? Because then women have been given the opportunity to show what they can do to cope with misfortunes of often catastrophic proportions. History richly demonstrates their effective responses to these events, within the family as well as in society. Consider what pioneer women did to establish homes and families across a new nation; the wives who struggled against unbelievable odds to keep homesteads going during the Civil War; the mothers who managed to provide for their families during the bleak Depression years. Nor is this a matter of past history. What about the wives of the men who fought in the Korean War, or in Vietnam?

Evidence of this kind has surely shattered forever the sentimental Victorian image of wives as weak, simpering creatures who fainted at the sight of a mouse. The modern wife expects to be a comrade to her husband, sharing the hard knocks, the dire disasters, and the tough predicaments which are the stuff of life, in the home and outside it. The evidence is mounting that the female of the species, far from being weak, incompetent, and helplessly dependent, can match and even outperform the male in endurance, in fortitude, in toughness—even in sexual performance! This is all very hard on the male ego, but in the long run he really has no option but to capitulate and to cooperate in working out new marriage patterns based on the comradeship which more and more wives now expect. John Scanzoni, in his thoughtful book *Sexual Bargaining: Power Politics in the American Marriage*[7] is probably right when he says that this struggle for a new alignment of men's and womens' roles is a crisis that will pass and will open the door to far more satisfying marriages for both sexes.

3. One of the unequivocal purposes of marriage through the centuries has been procreation. In the very large families in the centuries before our present one, marriage did indeed discriminate against women, even to the death. Vast numbers of young wives died in childbirth or worn out by too prolific child-bearing, only to be replaced, after a suitable lapse of time, by other young women willing to walk the same treadmill.

Today all this has changed. Can we therefore now say that marriage is good for women because they can choose how many children they have, or, if they listen to the ardent supporters of world population control, have none at all? Answers to that question may vary, but the fact that modern marriage does give such options to young wives and husbands surely

[7] John Scanzoni, *Sexual Bargaining: Power Politics in the American Marriage* (Englewood Cliffs, N.J.: Prentice-Hall, 1972).

removes a form of discrimination that was all the more deadly for being so subtle.

4. One of the most sensitive areas in any consideration of marriage discriminating against women focuses on who does the so-called "dirty" work? This becomes a major issue because it is so constant, so repetitive, so much of a grind to many wives (and some husbands).

There is an idea abroad that some women in the past had it better in this area because they had servants and slaves, not to mention older children and resident dependents, to help with the chores. This is a fallacy. What is overlooked is that large families of both close relatives and dependent helpers (as servants and slaves were) created vast responsibilities for feeding, clothing, nurturing, nursing during ill-health, and generally caring for all their members. On whom did the burden of these responsibilities mainly fall? On the married woman whose husband was the head of the family. If her household did not include helpers, did she escape this burden? No, because the chances were that she worked shoulder to shoulder, and very hard, with her menfolk on their small plot of land.

Did the lady of the large plantation and the lady of the small farm feel that marriage was bad for them because it involved hard work? We think not, and we find it reassuring to remember this when young wives complain today, forgetful of the fact that they have hundreds of aids to easier housekeeping that were denied to women in earlier generations.

But when all improvements are taken into account, plenty of disagreeable, unattractive chores remain. Is modern marriage unequal to that challenge? Certainly not. There are many examples of what married couples are doing about it. We think particularly of some personal friends—both busy professionals with children and a home to care for. They made a list of all the unattractive jobs in their home that neither wanted to do, discussed it thoroughly, and then divided

45

the items equally between them. Now they have an equitable and disciplined sharing of the grind with no discrimination anywhere except, as the husband points out, when either of them is absent from the house on professional assignment.

This enquiry appears to have unveiled one of those fortuitous situations in which investigation of the cause of the disease also opens up the trail leading to its cure. That women of the past have been discriminated against in marriage, to a shocking degree when judged by modern standards, cannot be denied. But modern standards are in fact the reflection of modern opportunities for a new and different kind of life, for women and men alike. And the process of reaping these new opportunities is beginning to remove instances of discrimination almost as quickly as we can identify and castigate them.

It is our considered opinion that the movement for women's liberation, which in most other respects we warmly support, has made a strategic error of major proportions in its bitter and ruthless attack on marriage. It is not in fact marriage itself that has been the enemy of woman's personhood, but the broader conditions of human society that allowed marriage to be used in past times both as an arena of discrimination and as an agent for its perpetuation.

Renouncing marriage and motherhood may indeed be for some women the path to fulfillment, and they should (and now do) have that option. But for the great majority of women the abandonment of marriage could be like the process of cutting off one's nose to spite one's face. It could even put them back where it all began and make them again the objects of exploitation by the predatory male. Complaints reflecting such exploitation have been frequent, both from hippie communes and from leftist groups.

What most women, and most men, need deeply is the kind of comradeship and shared life that marriage at its best makes possible. If marriage has been tolerated in the past at levels that were far below its best, that is no reason to continue to judge it solely in those terms—particularly now that new conditions open up the possibility of radical change.

It would seem to us (and we speak here from personal experience as well as from logical persuasion) that the true comradeship between men and women which we seek will not be fully achieved outside marriage until it is achieved in marriage and that once it is achieved extensively in marriage, its achievement outside marriage will be inevitable. What, after all, is holding back the cause of women's liberation? Mainly the stubborn opposition of men who, unwilling to accept an equal comradeship with their wives at home, therefore fear its implications in the wider life of the nation. And what, more than anything else, will change their minds? The discovery in their marriage that a wife no longer discriminated against becomes not a rampaging renegade, but a loyal partner and a trusted friend.

CHAPTER 5

A Reconstruction of the Marriage Scene

There has been an element of confusion in our discussion so far. You, the reader, may not have noticed it. We, the writers, have been painfully conscious of it. But we have tolerated it because it was our decision that this would serve our purpose best. Now the time has come to clear it up. This is for us one of the most important chapters in our whole book. We hope it will be like the *dénouement* in the detective story, when the bamboozled reader finally sees all the pieces neatly fitting together.

A few months before beginning to write this book we had the fascinating experience of leading a national workshop on the theme "The Meaning of the Man-Woman Relationship in the New Society." It was confined to about thirty-five professional men and women, was widely representative of many sections of society, and included such resourceful people as Carlfred Broderick, George and Nena O'Neill, and Herbert Otto. We talked together for a total of about ten hours, and the discussion was lively. It was a good experience for all who took part, and for us it was particularly significant because it enabled us to clear our minds on many controversial questions. Our own findings were not necessarily in all respects the same as those of the group, but here are the conclusions at which we personally arrived.

The notion is widespread that marriage today is being challenged, and may eventually be replaced, by looser and more

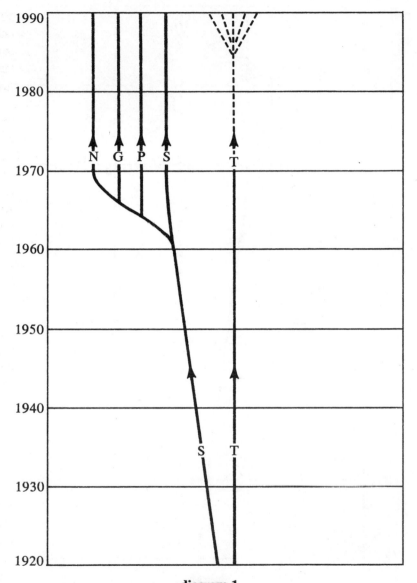

diagram 1
*Supposed Alternatives to Traditional
Marriage*

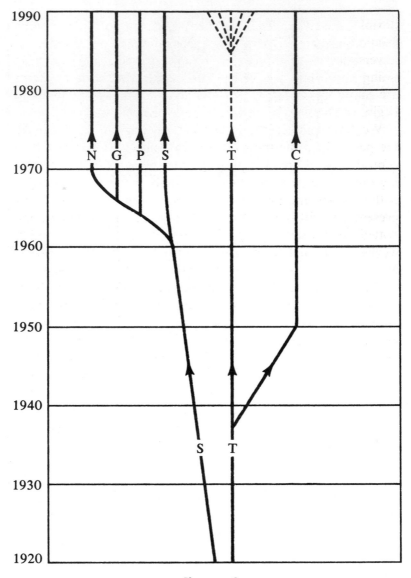

diagram 2
*Real Alternatives to Traditional
Marriage*

flexible life-styles. Two different concepts of man-woman relationship are alleged to be confronting one another as adversaries, with those who stand for traditional marriage lining up on one side while those who favor the freer forms are lining up on the other. The great tug-of-war is about to begin, and bets are being made as to which will win.

We have projected this concept in diagram 1. It covers the period of a lifetime—70 years, from 1920 to 1990. The central vertical line T represents traditional marriage, emerging out of the past, in which the family was viewed as rigid, authoritarian, and patriarchal. It continues its course into our present era, but is now beginning to falter, as shown by the dotted line. Future predictions see it as growing steadily weaker, and finally petering out altogether. This at any rate is what the "opposition" believes will happen.

To the left, we see the emerging new life-styles. They represent more flexible, open, relaxed patterns of man-woman interaction. The first of them was already emerging as an alternative to traditional marriage at the beginning of the century. It is serial or successive monogamy, and is marked S to distinguish it from traditional monogamy (lifelong union) to which it provided an alternative. It represents divorce and remarriage and is based on the view, often expressed, that one or more changes of marriage partner in a lifetime represents a more acceptable marriage pattern for many people.

Further to the left, and more recently promoted, is the alternative pattern P, which stands for plural marriage or polygamy. This represents the concept that a variety of marriage partners need not come in succession, but that a person of either sex could be married to more than one partner simultaneously. What we are considering here is a fairly stable polygamous association, of the type sometimes called multilateral marriage.

Further yet to the left is the variant G, which represents group marriage. Here the association with several partners is looser and freer than in P, but all of them consider themselves related to each other in some way—generally in the shared life of a commune.

A final alternative is N, which stands for no marriage at all—the decision not to enter into a relationship of any definable type, but to enjoy associations with the opposite sex as they come, with no commitment and no social recognition. What happens here is that the group of possible partners, limited in G, widens out to include potentially everyone, or at least every eligible person who is likely to be encountered in the course of a lifetime.

This wide range of choices, then, covers the various life-styles, which are seen as alternatives to traditional monogamy. The view frequently expressed is that in the future more and more people will break out of the narrow confines of the traditional pattern and orbit in the wide spaces occupied by these highly flexible variants.

This analysis of the alternatives before us has been very widely accepted and very extensively publicized. We are now convinced that it is grossly inaccurate, and that as a result the whole matter has been very much confused.

We therefore present diagram 2, which we consider to be the correct picture. It resembles diagram 1, with one very important addition. We now see a line emerging to the right of T—a departure from traditional marriage which began to be noted around the 1930s and predated the more recently recognized alternative life-styles, except that of serial monogamy. This line is C, which represents what we shall call the "companionship" marriage (not to be confused with the "companionate" marriage of Judge Ben Lindsay,[1] which was a very different concept).

Notice that the traditional marriage, portrayed by the cen-

---

[1] Ben B. Lindsay and Wainwright Evans, *The Companionate Marriage* (New York: Boni and Liveright, 1927). The book proposed to legalize trial marriages for young people and thereby raised a national furor.

tral vertical line T, is still represented as destined to peter out. We ourselves agree with the critics who predict that this closed, rigid, highly institutional pattern is becoming increasingly anachronistic and will in all probability cease to exist in our culture.

The point at which we do *not* agree with the critics is that we must choose between traditional marriage and the new lifestyles portrayed on the left. There is another very viable alternative in the form of the companionship marriage which has been available for some time and which millions of married couples have already chosen as *their* alternative. To mix the traditional marriage and the companionship marriage together in one package, as we have been doing, is a gross error, totally inaccurate and extremely confusing. This is the confusion we have tolerated in our discussion up to now in order to illustrate the point. When we spoke of marriage as it now exists, without further definition, there was no way of knowing what we were really referring to—something that is manifestly dying, or something else which we see as the real future of man-woman relationship. Henceforth this distinction must be absolutely clear, or everything we have to say in the rest of the book will be open to misinterpretation.

We are now ready to focus our attention on the companionship marriage. It was very fully studied and described by Ernest Burgess, the distinguished American family sociologist, and was judged to be a decisive departure from the traditional pattern. He summarized the transition in the phrase "from institution to companionship."

Let Burgess, and his colleague Harvey Locke, speak for themselves—"The central thesis of this volume is that the family in historical times has been, and at present is, in transition from an institution to a companionship. In the past the important factors unifying the family have been external, formal, and authoritarian, as the law, the mores, public opinion, tradition, the authority of the family head, rigid

53

discipline, and elaborate ritual. At present, in the new emerging form of the companionship family, its unity inheres less and less in community pressures and more and more in such interpersonal relationships as the mutual affection, the sympathetic understanding, and the comradeship of its members." [2] These are the opening words of the preface by Burgess and Locke to their monumental, eight-hundred-page volume *The Family.* The book, first published in 1945, has been viewed by family sociologists as a classical work describing the breakaway of the new democratic family from the old authoritarian family.

What then happened to this new democratic, companionship type of marriage? Why do we never hear about it in the current debate? Why is the book by Burgess and Locke not even listed by the O'Neills in the bibliography of about a hundred titles appended to their best-selling volume *Open Marriage?* [3]

This is an important question. The contrast described by Burgess and Locke delineates very accurately the direction in which our culture is traveling. Consider the words used to describe the traditional, institutional marriage pattern—"formal, authoritarian, authority of the family head, rigid discipline, elaborate ritual." Surely these are precisely the family values against which women's lib and the new lifestyles are in revolt. Then consider the words used to describe the new emerging marriage pattern—"interpersonal relationships, mutual affection, sympathetic understanding, comradeship." Surely these are the very qualities in relationships being emphasized by the new generation and the counter culture. Yet today's parents, accused bitterly by their teen-aged children of lacking just those qualities, were moving toward mar-

[2] Ernest W. Burgess and Harvey J. Locke, *The Family: From Institution to Companionship* (New York: American Book Company, 1945).

[3] Nena and George O'Neill, *Open Marriage: A New Life-Style for Couples* (New York: Evans, 1972).

riage at the very time when the Burgess findings were being announced.

What went wrong? We will venture to offer an explanation. We ourselves have lived and worked through those critical years and have been increasingly disquieted. The concept of the companionship marriage *did* emerge. Those of us who taught marriage courses, besides accepting it for ourselves, presented it diligently to our students; and the students received it eagerly. It was written up in books and in magazine articles. It represented an ideal that was totally in keeping with the best American values, and this is still the case.

Many American marriages today are living demonstrations of that ideal. The couples concerned have broken with the traditional, authoritarian, rigid, institutional pattern. They are deeply in love with one another, and enjoy warm, happy, confiding relationships with their children. Husbands and wives are dedicated to a fully equalitarian acceptance of each other. They are quietly living out the kind of marriage young people in love dream about. They provide living proof that truly happy marriages are entirely possible.

But for many more American couples, the dream has not come true. They are disillusioned, bitter, and exhibit vividly in their broken hopes the spectacle of marriage as slavery, as exploitation, as a cruel counterfeit. It is they who in their words and actions have spoken loudly to the younger generation, convincing many of them that marriage is a shambles and they had better look for workable alternatives. To that younger generation, the message of the happily married silent minority has almost completely failed to get through.

Why have so many failed? The answer is very simple and very clear. The transition from the traditional marriage to the companionship marriage is far from easy. In many respects it represents a reversal of values and of roles. It is a whole new way of life. And, as we discovered with our students, it took a lot of teaching, a lot of help and guidance and counseling,

55

to enable them to make the transition. But, given the help they needed, most of them made it.

The great majority of the American people have never been given that help. They have tried to be companions in marriage and have ended up being adversaries. In their effort to give up the authoritarian approach to raising their children, they have swung wildly to the opposite extreme, and ended up with an indulgent permissiveness that turned those children into rebels. They wanted to make the transition, and most of them tried, but they simply lacked the knowledge and skill to do it and ended in confusion or in the divorce court. It was just too difficult.

The critics are right. The traditional marriage is an anachronism and will not survive in our new, open society. But the critics are entirely wrong in concluding that we have nothing to put in its place and that we must now think up new alternatives. The thinking has already been done, and the theory has been tested and found to be sound and healthy. There are millions of American homes where the alternative is working magnificently. But these happy, successful companionship marriages get no publicity. No press reporters interview them, no magazines write them up. They are the silent, overlooked, unidentified minority.

What is worst of all is that, in the inaccurate analysis that most of us have accepted, these companionship marriages are just lumped in with the mass of traditional marriages. It is not simply that they are not being noticed. They are being counted in as part of the marriage system which they have renounced as decisively as have the advocates of the more colorful life-styles. The reason for this is of course that the breakaway in one case has taken place quietly, gradually, and unobtrusively while in the other case it has been shouted from the housetops. It is as if two alienated sons both left home—the elder moving quietly into separate quarters and starting a new life on his own, the other publicly denouncing his parents as tyrannical and getting the whole shocking story written up in the local newspaper.

We are dealing, therefore, not with one but with two alternatives to the traditional marriage, both of which have broken away from the original parent stock. How can they be compared to each other?

We shall have a great deal to say later about the companionship marriage; but let us indicate clearly now how it differs from the new life-styles. As we have seen, what unites the latter is that they are all based on the belief that marriages are failing today primarily because the bond is too close, so that it stifles the growth and individuality of the partners. The battle cry of the advocates of these new patterns is "make the relationship looser and more open, and all will be well."

The companionship marriage is based on the very opposite view. We hold that the reason for the failure of the traditional marriage in our modern world is not that the relationship is too close, but that it is not close enough. We grew up in the time when traditional marriages were universal, and we saw plenty of them. Within the tight structure of the rigid institution, most of these couples lived a long way apart from each other. Their relationships were highly formal, and often very superficial. They were held together by pressure from the outside, by the sense of duty imposed upon the partners, and by the fear of retribution if they broke up. So when in our less rigid society the outside pressures were taken off, there was very little to keep them intact. It is not surprising that their descendants found the system unworkable and began to abandon it.

We believe that the solution to our marital ailments lies exactly in the opposite direction to the one in which we are looking. What will make marriage happy and fulfilling is bringing the couple closer together in an in-depth relationship that makes possible the creative sharing of life. The boredom of which so many married couples complain springs not from their being too close together but too far apart. It is not the tight bond, but the empty space, that leads to disillusionment.

We have now completed our brief investigation of modern marriage from the outside, as a unit of society. Our next task is to look at marriage from the inside, as an intimate interpersonal relationship.

PART II

Marriage Viewed from the Inside

CHAPTER 6

How Marriage Has Changed

"Marriage in the past was held together by external coercion. Today it can be held together only by internal cohesion."

This statement was made by one of us many years ago, and we have often used it since. It sums up neatly the revolutionary change that has taken place—a change which we *must* understand clearly if we are to make modern marriages work.

The nature of the change can be well understood by looking at diagram 3. What it illustrates is the fact that marriage has literally been turned inside out.

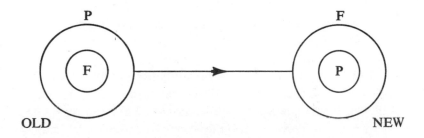

P   F

F   P

OLD   NEW

The Changing Pattern of Marriage

Look first at the old pattern on the left. The space within the outer circle represents the marriage. The inner circle (the bull's eye) represents the central goal of the marriage. In the old pattern, this is indicated by the letter F, which stands for familial obligations and duties. Out on the circumference, far from the central goal, we find the letter P, which stands for personal fulfillment.

What this means should be quite clear. In the old days, the primary purpose of marriage was to carry out the family duties—having children to continue the ancestral name and line, taking care of the family land and property, preserving the family tradition. We still retain some relics of this old concept of family continuity—a familiar one is the custom, when a son is born, of giving him the same name as his father—John Smith, Jr. Another is the tradition, at weddings, which required the father to "give away" his daughter—separating her off from his own family so that she could now devote herself to building up the family of her husband.

Still, in many parts of the world, this old concept lives on. In the Orient parents still arrange marriages—choosing husbands for their daughters and wives for their sons, sometimes without consulting the young people at all. In old Japanese weddings, when the marriage certificate was signed, it was the patriarchs of the two families, not the bride and bridegroom, who put their signatures to the document. The marriage was a contract completed between the two families. The young people were simply pawns—pawns used to negotiate an interfamily alliance.

There was, of course, always the hope that the marriage would bring personal happiness to the husband and wife. But that was of minor importance. What mattered was that children should be born—specially sons to continue the family name. The relationship between the couple was something quite superficial. In some extended families they didn't even live together, but in the men's and women's quarters respectively.

Now consider the marriages of today. If we look at the diagram representing the new pattern, we see that the positions of the F and the P have been reversed. Now the main goal of marriage is personal fulfillment, and family duties are considered less important.

If you want to test this out, ask any engaged couple why they are getting married. They may find the question surprising and even consider it impertinent because it's a question we don't usually ask. So you may have to spell it out and say, "Well, for instance, are you getting married to carry on the family tradition?" This may puzzle them further still, and they may have to admit that such an idea had never even entered their heads. In the end they will probably get impatient and say, "Look, we're getting married because we're in love and because we hope to be happy together."

Of course. That's why people get married today. And it probably never occurs to them that it's an entirely different reason from the one for which people were married in older times and in older cultures. In that sense, marriage really has been turned inside out.

This radical change has made marriage a great deal more complicated. It was comparatively easy to make the old-time marriage work. The main thing was to have sexual intercourse and get the wife pregnant. That wasn't too difficult for the average man, especially when the wife wasn't expected to respond, because it was unladylike for a woman to enjoy sex. Beyond that, no intimacies were expected. The husband's duties were clearly defined. He did the outside jobs and a few technical tasks and occasional heavy lifting indoors. The wife was in complete charge of the home. Her responsibilities were the cooking, the cleaning, the mending, the care of the children, and perhaps a little gardening. Their roles kept them apart, and they didn't get in each other's way. If any disagreement arose between them, the husband could settle it swiftly by exerting his authority as the head of the house. Those old marriages could be very superficial and still keep going because they were mainly motivated by a sense of duty. Divorce was either impossible to get or considered a disgrace to the family; so it was best to jog along and make the best of it.

Undoubtedly, however, some of those marriages were very happy—as good as the best marriages of today. But this was not essential. If it happened, it was a welcome bonus. If it didn't, the situation was accepted with a shrug of the shoulders.

By contrast, look at today's marriage. It *has* to bring happiness, or else. It is undertaken for love, so it is expected that it will all go smoothly and sweetly. The sex life must measure up to high requirements. There must be good companionship, so disagreements are very painful. When they arise, they aren't easily settled because this is an equal partnership, so each partner has one vote. How do you settle the question when each votes differently?

We once made a study of marriage in Asia, and wrote a book called *Marriage: East and West* [1] which compared the two patterns. The most striking difference we found was in the area of *expectations*. In the East, expectations of marriage are relatively low; consequently they are fairly easily fulfilled, and contentment usually results. In the West, by contrast, expectations are so high that in most cases they can't reasonably be met, so some degree of disillusionment is almost inevitable.

The failure of the partner to measure up to expectations is all the more distressing when people marry for love, as they do today. If you choose your mate, you pride yourself on your selection; so you are particularly annoyed if your choice turns out to have been unwise. Lord Beaconsfield, who lived in England in the days when the love match was first beginning to be accepted, is quoted as saying, "All my friends who have married for love and beauty either beat their wives or live apart from them. This is literally the case. I may commit many follies in life, but I never intend to marry for love." [2]

There are other complications, too. In earlier times people almost always married a partner from some neighboring family, and the pair started life together with a great deal in common—the same basic education, the same religion, the same social background, the same values. Sociological studies

---

[1] Mace, *Marriage: East and West,* pp. 294-96.
[2] André Maurois in *Disraeli* (London: John Lane, 1927), p. 67.

64

have shown again and again that a common social background makes for the most stable marriages. Today, however, people often marry who are out of very different backgrounds with very different values and standards. Such marriages can be challenging and very successful, but the amount of adjustment each must make to the other is greatly increased.

In addition, people today live under great stress. The pace of life is swift and sometimes furious. It is often quite hard for married couples to find the leisure, and the detachment, to cultivate their companionship. And in our mobile population, with the average family moving every five years, the support of familiar surroundings, dependable relatives, and trusted friends is often lacking in times of crisis.

What this all adds up to is that marriage today is a very much more difficult task than it was in the past. Indeed, it is so difficult that large numbers of otherwise quite competent and intelligent people fail to find it satisfying and become disenchanted.

Yet many of these people need not fail. We are convinced, from our long years of experience in marriage counseling, that there is a great deal of needless frustration and unhappiness in modern marriage. The source of most of our trouble lies in our irrational attitude. Out of ignorance or stubbornness or pride or culpable indifference or for some other reason, we will not acknowledge, once and for all, the fact that *marriage today can be very rewarding, but is also very difficult; and the rewards come only to those who recognize that success in it calls for as much intelligence and skill as success in a career or in any other major enterprise.*

If only we could all take hold firmly of this well-established fact and act on it, the proportion of successful marriages might soon begin to show a phenomenal increase.

CHAPTER 7

Marriage Is What You Make It

There is no possible doubt that we can have better marriages if we want them enough. So the question we have to ask is *do* we want them? Is marriage really a necessity for our well-being?

In the past, as we have seen, it was a social necessity. It would not be profitable to argue about whether the human race could have developed apart from the family, any more than it is to speculate about what would have happened if babies had really been delivered by storks. The family has been central to mankind throughout recorded history, and the available evidence strongly suggests that it played a central role during the two million years before that. Indeed, it has its roots way back in subhuman species—there are bird families and animal families as well as human families.

But is the situation different today? Yes, in many respects it is. The main function of the family has been to produce and raise children. Producing them is relatively easy—raising them is another matter. Technically, we may be near the point at which they can be produced in test tubes; although there is no particular value in that, since women generally are not averse to the experience of motherhood. The really complex and vital task is *rearing* children. And this could be done by specially appointed people with special aptitude for parenthood—professional upbringers they might be called. This

66

would not be very different from our present system of foster parents. It would clearly be workable.

In other words, if people in large numbers declined to marry and set up homes, this would not now be a major disaster from the point of view of human survival. Alternative means could, and obviously would, be provided for replenishing the population. So the absolute necessity of the family from a social point of view no longer exists.

But of course this is only intellectual discussion. Although there is loud talk of motherhood being a doomed profession, there is no evidence that either women or men in our culture, in any significant numbers, have lost all interest in raising children. Parenthood can be a very fulfilling human experience, and it hardly seems likely that we are about to abandon it.

Moreover, marriage offers substantial rewards quite apart from parenthood. Couples who find themselves childless don't decide that there's no point in going on with their marriages. In fact, studies have found that satisfying marriages occur slightly more frequently among childless couples than among those with children. So marriage for its own sake, quite apart from children, meets some pretty basic human needs. And this goes much deeper than the traditional need a woman had to find a man to protect and support her or a man's need for a woman to run his home and sew on his buttons. These utilitarian reasons for marriage have lost a good deal of validity in recent years, and yet people have gone on marrying on an unprecedented scale.

We can, if we like, give the urge to marry a technical name and call it pair-bonding, as Desmond Morris[1] does. A better way is to spell it out in terms of human friendship and to see marriage as a deep and satisfying sharing of life between two people who combine the comradeship of equals with the com-

[1] Desmond Morris, *The Human Zoo* (New York: McGraw-Hill, 1969), pp. 83-84.

plementarity of the sexes. We know of no statement that has ever expressed this better than one made by Edward Carpenter way back in 1911 in his delightful but now little-known book *Love's Coming-of-Age.*

That there should exist one other person in the world toward whom all openness of interchange should establish itself, from whom there should be no concealment; whose body should be as dear to one, in every part, as one's own; with whom there should be no sense of Mine or Thine, in property or possession; into whose mind one's thoughts should naturally flow, as it were to know themselves and to receive a new illumination; and between whom and oneself there should be a spontaneous rebound of sympathy in all the joys and sorrows and experiences of life; such is perhaps one of the dearest wishes of the soul.[2]

We believe this to be a classical statement of the motivations that lead people to marry. Not many people would be able to command such language. Some would not even be consciously aware of what they were seeking. Yet most of us, reading and rereading that statement until its full meaning is clear to us, would respond from the depth of our hearts: "Yes, that's what I want; and I would give a great deal to get it."

It's interesting to notice that even writers who attack marriage tend to be ambivalent about it. Kathrin Perutz, for example, declares that marriage is hell, yet concludes her preface with these words: "Here, then, is a book about marriage as hell by someone who has inhabited the place long enough to recognize it as home." [3] The ambivalence is dramatized in a statement made by a woman patient to a well-known psychotherapist to the effect that all men are brutal, selfish, and inconsiderate, and she wished she could find one.

In other words, it is bad marriage that is being attacked,

[2] Edward Carpenter, *Love's Coming-of-Age* (New York: Mitchell Kennerley, 1911), pp. 99-100.
[3] Perutz, *Marriage Is Hell*, p. viii.

the supposition being that bad marriage is well-nigh universal. The proposal to abandon marriage, therefore, seems to be prompted not so much by opposition to marriage in principle, as by the conviction that it won't work in practice.

In this discussion we are not saying that marriage is necessary or desired by all people. Edward Carpenter, in the book from which we have quoted, says: "There are millions of people today who never could marry happily—however favorable the conditions might be." [4] And we are not forgetting Westermarck's pertinent observation that "marriage is not made for everybody, not attractive to everybody, nor good for everybody who embarks on it." [5] What we *are* saying is that marriage still meets deep personal needs which large numbers of people cannot satisfy in any other way.

Some people are by nature loners and seem to have little need of human companionship. But the great majority of us are deeply dependent for our satisfactions on the warm, reassuring approval and support of others. Being married does not exclude other friendships in our lives, of course; but there is something very reassuring and supportive about having one special comrade at whose side you have fought a thousand battles and shared a thousand achievements, whom you can trust completely, and with whom you can be totally open and relaxed.

There are those who say they do not need this depth of relationship, or that it is not precious enough in their eyes to justify the price that has to be paid for it. They see more reward in the sum total of a number of relationships which, added together, can in their judgment equal one sustained relationship of great depth. They suggest that their own personality development will be better furthered by a kaleidoscopic series of encounters with many others than by putting "all their eggs in one basket."

[4] Carpenter, *Love's Coming-of-Age*, p. 118.
[5] Westermarck, *The History of Human Marriage*, p. 31.

Those people must make their own choices. Our culture should not impose marriage on anybody; and it is no part of our purpose in life to persuade anyone to choose marriage. We believe, however, that the great majority of people, when they have weighed the issues, want to live within the married state. And this being so, we want them to have enough understanding of the task that lies before them to assure them of the best possible chance of achieving success in it.

Why have so many people, recognizing their need for what marriage has to offer, married and then suffered disillusionment because their need was not met? What went wrong?

At least one whole generation of young people have been fed a lot of romantic nonsense. The fairy tale story of the prince and princess who were married after the most superficial acquaintance, rode off together into the sunset, and contrived to live happily ever after still dominates our fantasies. Otherwise we would have more sense than to marry with little or no preparation, assume after marriage that everything would go fine with little or no need to make adjustments in our ways of thinking and behaving, and devote less attention to the maintenance of our marriages than to the upkeep of our cars or our homes.

We simply must abandon the ridiculous and iniquitous ideas we have nurtured about marriage which suggest that romantic love is all you need to achieve happiness and harmony in the most complex and demanding of all human relationships. Surely by this time enough evidence has been piled up to prove conclusively that this is far from the truth!

So long as people enter marriage with the idea that they are weighing anchor in a protected haven where no storms can come, they are almost inevitably doomed to disappointment. Getting married is much more like a ship putting out to sea and bracing itself to meet the tempests that await it over the horizon. The land of heart's desire is not where the couple are now. It lies far ahead, and it will take all the skill and unfaltering resolution they can muster to reach it.

The reason for this is obvious when you give the matter a little serious thought. What *is* marriage? In terms of what we are asking today, it is a close, intimate relationship in which two people share life on a very broad basis and in great depth. They live together, eat together, dress and undress together, sleep together, have sex together. This adds up to a degree of intimacy not found in any other continuing human relationship. In addition to this, they enter into a partnership in which they run a joint home, manage their money in common, share the responsibility of raising their children, establish common relationships with relatives, friends, neighbors, business colleagues, tradesmen, and the world in general. Their individual actions and projects must be planned in relation to each other's wishes, powers, and capacities for tolerance. They must also cope together with any number of crises—illness, financial problems, vocational changes, difficulties with children and between children, breakdown of plans, and natural disasters. This is obviously only a partial list. No other cooperative enterprise between persons, on a sustained basis, can approximate the degree of mutual involvement which marriage requires.

In other words, the couple have to *accept marriage as a task*—a task at which both husband and wife must work together. Edward Carpenter, immediately following his classical passage on the ideal marriage, goes on: "It is obvious that this state of affairs cannot be reached at a single leap, but must be the gradual result of years of intertwined memory and affection. For such a union love must lay the foundation, but patience and gentle consideration and self-control must work unremittingly to perfect the structure." [6]

Don Jackson, a brilliant psychiatrist who studied the dy-

[6] Carpenter, *Love's Coming-of-Age,* p. 100.

namics of marital interaction by analyzing what he saw happening to hundreds of couples, summed up his conclusion in plain language: "Relationship is a process involving constant change; and constant change requires the spouses to *keep working on their relationship until the day they die.*" [7] Abigail Van Buren ("Dear Abby"), a marriage expert of a different kind, agrees: "How does a woman make a good marriage great?" she asks, "That's easy. She simply works like a dog at it!" [8]

We hope we have made our point, clearly and plainly. Marriage has a great deal to offer, but it is not a magic kingdom where the usual principles don't apply and where you get something for nothing. The sooner we kill that lie, the better for all concerned.

[7] William J. Lederer and Don D. Jackson, *The Mirages of Marriage* (New York: W. W. Norton, 1968), p. 199.

[8] Abigail Van Buren, "How to Make a Good Marriage Great," *Family Circle,* Nov., 1971.

CHAPTER 8

Involvement Is the Word

Yes, you have to work at marriage. We don't take back a word we have said on that subject. But something must be added, and it is of great importance. You have to work at your marriage *intelligently.*

We have known married people ready indeed to work like dogs, and until the day they die. Yet the results of their efforts were not spectacular because those efforts were not applied at the right points or in the right manner. They remind us of the saying about the man who jumped on his horse and rode off in all directions.

The recipe for success in marriage, therefore, is for *effort plus insight.* Effort without insight won't do it; and insight without effort won't do it. The combination of both is what succeeds.

There's something else that we had better say now, too, before we go any further. We have made it clear that there are a few people (only a few, we think) for whom marriage has nothing to offer and who had better leave it alone. In addition to these, however, there are people who want and need what marriage has to offer, but they are blocked by personality difficulties from achieving their goal. These difficulties rob them of the capacity for the necessary effort, or the necessary insight, or both. Such people need individual counseling or psychotherapy in order to free them inwardly to be able to meet the demands of a close relationship.

73

Now we must concentrate on the matter of insight. By this we mean understanding what it is you have to do in order to live comfortably and creatively in a close relationship with another person of the opposite sex. Up to now the assumption has been that anybody can do this, that it requires no special knowledge or skill.

This is far from the truth. In the traditional marriage all relationships between men and women were hierarchically structured. A man's role in marriage was to be the head, to take charge, to issue orders, and to make decisions. A woman's role was to do what she was told, to treat her husband with respect even when she didn't agree with him, to suppress her feelings of hostility and resentment in order to keep the peace. The older couples who provided us with our marriage models all accepted this in principle.

Now the pattern has been changed. What we accept in principle today is the companionship marriage, which makes the man and woman equal partners. However, most of us run into difficulties when we try to make it work in practice. One important reason for this is that so far we have very few models to demonstrate to us just how it is done. As Rudolfh Dreikurs perceptively pointed out. "There is no tradition that teaches us how to live with each other as equals, in mutual respect and trust." [1] And since most of our learning about how to behave is based on our largely unconscious observation of how others behave, this is a serious handicap. There is no alternative, in the circumstances, but for us to learn it consciously, translate our knowledge into insight as we apply it to our own life experience and build the new models which the new generation needs.

The analogy of automobile manufacture may help us here. Once a basic car design has been found workable and tooling

[1] Rudolfh Dreikurs in *The Marriage Relationship: Psychoanalytic Perspectives,* Salo Rosenbaum and Ian Algo, eds. (New York: Basic Books, 1968), p. 103.

up completed, copies of the successful prototype can be run off on the assembly line in large numbers. However, when a radical design change is called for, major problems must be overcome. Marriage is undergoing a radical design change right now.

At the heart of the new companionship marriage lies the desire of both partners for intimacy, closeness, and the deep sharing of life experiences. This couldn't be a goal in the old type of marriage because the dominance of the husband and the submissiveness of the wife placed them on different levels so that they had to look up or down, and not across, at each other. The sharp division of their spheres of interest, also, made it unwise for them to interfere in each other's lives. We found an extreme instance of this in an elderly couple in Tokyo, who are now grandparents. They had lived in the same house during their entire married life; and, believe it or not, the husband had *never* been in the kitchen. "That is my wife's province," he explained, "and I would never interfere with her work in the house, just as she would never interfere in my business."

The word that best sums up the change is "involvement." When two people become involved, it means that they cross the frontier that separates them from one another and enter to some extent into each other's private lives. This provides the intimacy and closeness for which most of us yearn, because the vast impersonal urban world in which we now live makes us feel small, lonely, unimportant, and often worthless. Sharing life deeply with another, and being loved, trusted, and appreciated even when we are fully known, gives us back a sense of identity and self-confidence. This was of course what Edward Carpenter wrote about, and our need for it has increased rather than diminished since his time.

Here is a diagram that illustrates different degrees of involvement between marriage partners.

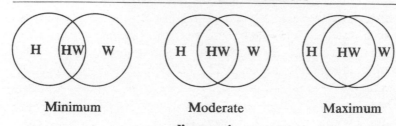

| Minimum | Moderate | Maximum |

diagram 4

Degrees of Involvement in Marriage

The circles with H and W represent husband and wife. You will see that they overlap very little in the first diagram, about halfway in the second, and very much in the third. The three represent respectively marriages of minimum involvement, of moderate involvement, and of maximum involvement. Let's see what this means.

In the marriage of minimum involvement husband and wife live separate lives as far as this is consistent with their being married to each other. In the traditional type of low involvement marriage, the husband provides his wife with the housekeeping money and leaves all questions of home management to her. He spends most of his spare time busy with his own interests and hobbies. The wife doesn't bother him, unless it is absolutely necessary, with household matters or problems concerning the children. She does what she has to do in the home and otherwise pursues her own personal interests. Husband and wife don't talk much about their interests and activities. They seldom do pleasurable things together or share their deeper thoughts and feelings. Their sex life is perfunctory. They don't think of each other often. Their relationship is based on an exchange of services; they have few quarrels and few moments of tenderness.

This kind of marriage need not be judged unsuccessful. Many traditional marriages were of this type. It represents all that some people want or expect in marriage. If both partners feel the same way about it, they may both be quite

76

satisfied. By keeping at a distance from each other the couple avoid many troubles that make other marriages miserable.

In the marriage of maximum involvement, by contrast, the couple want to share their lives as fully as they can. The husband is deeply interested in his wife's world and she in his. They like to do things together whenever possible, and they share all the roles involved in marriage as far as they can. Their thoughts and feelings are open to one another, and they talk a great deal together about what is going on in their inner and outer lives. They cooperate closely in the running of the home, the raising of the children, the management of their finances. All major decisions are made together. Disagreements between them are faced and worked through until they arrive at a solution fully acceptable to both. They are warmly supportive of each other in times of trouble. They respect and trust each other with understanding and tolerance. Their love for each other is expressed freely in tender, affectionate exchanges.

The marriage of moderate involvement lies somewhere between these extremes. Most American marriages fall into this category. Since marriage is usually pictured as a close and intimate love relationship, this is what couples aim for in the beginning. But they find the going hard and eventually settle for less somewhere along the continuum.

Again, this can be quite acceptable. If husband and wife are both reasonably contented with their relationship as it has turned out, it can be called a satisfactory marriage. It could even be called a happy marriage. However, the word "happy" is used so loosely to describe marriages that it has become almost meaningless. A couple can put on a show of superficial affability in public when in fact their marriage is miserably unhappy. Another couple can quarrel with each other in the presence of others and yet be entirely happy about their relationship. The situation in which serious trouble develops is when the level of involvement desired by the wife and that desired by the husband are far apart. Unfortunately this is a very common situation frequently encountered by marriage counselors.

The concept of involvement, then, is central to the companionship marriage. It is the center of our hopes and expectations; and it is the arena in which our problems have to be faced and resolved. We shall discuss this in more detail in the next chapter.

CHAPTER 9

The Meaning of Intimacy

We are now confronted with the central dilemma of marriage today. The more mutual involvement you want in a relationship, the higher the price you have to pay for it.

Imagine two people confined together in a square field, each side a mile long. They could coexist fairly well. If they wanted to talk, they could easily get together. If one wanted the other's help, he could be easily located. If on the other hand they wanted to be alone, or had had a quarrel, they could quickly get out of sight and sound of each other.

Now start shrinking the living space of these two people. Make the sides half a mile—still there would be plenty of room. Quarter of a mile—still adequate space. But reduce the area to one hundred fifty square feet—the area of an average bedroom—and you have a very different situation. Now these two people would be fully conscious of each other during every waking moment. Each would see every move the other made, would hear every cough, every sneeze, every grunt, every groan. Privacy would virtually be gone; escape would be impossible. They would be shut up together in a state of unavoidable intimacy. A disagreement now would be much more painful, much more difficult to resolve. No chance to cool off, to get away and gain new perspective, to look at the situation objectively.

That's what intimacy means—great when the two people are in harmony with one another, terrible when they're in conflict.

This inherent contradiction at the heart of marriage has been well understood in many cultures. It is beautifully expressed in an old Indian legend which describes how Twashtri, the Creator, ran into trouble when he made woman to be a companion to man.

In the beginning, when Twashtri came to the creation of woman, he found that he had exhausted his materials in the making of man, and that no solid elements were left. In this dilemma, after profound meditation, he did as follows. He took the rotundity of the moon, and the curves of the creepers, and the clinging of tendrils, and the trembling of grass, and the slenderness of the reed, and the bloom of flowers, and the lightness of leaves, and the tapering of the elephant's trunk, and the glances of deer, and the clustering of rows of bees, and the joyous gaiety of sunbeams, and the weeping of clouds, and the fickleness of the winds, and the timidity of the hare, and the vanity of the peacock, and the softness of the parrot's bosom, and the hardness of adamant, and the sweetness of honey, and the cruelty of the tiger, and the warm glow of the fire, and the coldness of snow, and the chattering of jays, and the cooing of the *Kokila,* and the hypocrisy of the crane, and the fidelity of the *chakrawaka;* and compounding all these together he made woman, and gave her to man. But after one week, man came to him and said: "Lord, this creature that you have given me makes my life miserable. She chatters incessantly, and teases beyond endurance, never leaving me alone: and she requires incessant attention, and takes all my time up, and cries about nothing and is always idle: and so I have come to give her back again as I cannot live with her." So Twashtri said: "Very well." And he took her back. Then after another week man came again to him and said: "Lord, I find that my life is very lonely since I gave you back that creature. I remember how she used to dance and sing to me, and play with me, and cling to me; and her laughter was music, and she was beautiful to look at, and soft to touch: so give her back to me again." So Twashtri said: "Very well." And he gave her back again. Then after only three days, man came back to him again, and said: "Lord, I know not how it is: but after all, I have come to the conclusion that she is more of a trouble than a pleasure to me: so please take her back again." But Twashtri said: "Out on you! Be off! I will have no more of this. You must manage how you can." The man said: "But I cannot live with her." And Twashtri replied: "Neither could you live without her." And he turned his back on man, and went on with his work. The man said: "What is to be done? For I cannot live either with or without her." [1]

Everyone who has been married understands the man's dilemma—"I cannot live either with her or without her." And it is of course equally true for the woman.

This then is the basic problem that confronts all married couples as they seek deeper levels of involvement. They become aware of forces drawing them toward one another (attraction) and other forces driving them apart (repulsion). We could call these forces affinities and hostilities. However, we shouldn't conclude from this that the hostilities are evil forces because this isn't true. Actually, they are *protective* forces. They guard the inner sanctuary of our individuality. They prevent us from becoming *too* involved with another person, which could be damaging to both.

We often speak of marriage as a union of two personalities. This is confusing because the word has two different meanings. If we mean by union an association for mutual benefit, like the union of the states in the United States, that is an excellent description of marriage. But if we mean, as we sometimes do, that the two become one in a sort of fusion of personalities, that is foolish, sentimental nonsense. It is true that the Bible speaks of marriage as two becoming one, but the reference there is to the "flesh," which means sexual union. It is also true that, in the past, English law viewed the married couple

[1] Quoted by Howard L. Philp in *A Psychologist Looks at Sex* (London: Hutchinson, 1945), p. 75.

as one person—which meant that the wife's identity was lost by being merged, for legal purposes, with her husband. But the concept of two personalities being fused together would be quite intolerable because it would mean the destruction of the identity of each. Against this the ego would fight to the death—and that is exactly what happens when two people seek intimacy beyond their tolerance.

Dr. Van de Velde, author of the first best-selling marriage manual, *Ideal Marriage,*[2] published in 1936 another book, almost unknown today, entitled *Sex Hostility In Marriage.*[3] It was intended to supplement in the psychological area what the author had been teaching couples about the physical side of marriage. It was in fact a book about interpersonal intimacy between husband and wife. The mistake the author made was to put all the emphasis on what he believed to be a deep, natural aversion between the sexes that surfaces in marriage as mutual hostility. No doubt there *are* gender differences that can hinder a man and woman in making a total commitment to each other. But a far more important explanation of hostility in marriage, in our opinion, is the invasion of privacy which can result from a close relationship between any two people regardless of their gender.

This question has become a very important one today because of our great emphasis on individual identity and freedom. It was vividly illustrated for us in a conversation with a talented young woman of twenty-six who told us that she would never marry. She went on to explain that while she wanted and needed intimacy, she felt it was best to get this in a series of relationships with men that could each be broken off before it began to interfere with her personal freedom to be herself. We told her that we saw in this a self-defeating pattern that could only lead to a succession of frustrations of

[2] Th. H. de Velde, *Ideal Marriage* (New York: Random House, 1928).
[3] Th. H. de Velde, *Sex Hostility in Marriage* (London: Heinemann, 1936).

her need for intimacy without contributing anything to her need for freedom. A long and very interesting discussion followed.

We can well understand this fear of intimacy in marriage in the light of what has happened in the past. The exponents of women's liberation are right when they speak of the brutal subjection of woman's personhood in patriarchal cultures. We want no more of that. And the companionship marriage which Burgess saw beginning to emerge renounces this feature of traditional marriage as vehemently as does the women's liberation movement. It does not, however, make the foolish mistake of renouncing marriage itself in the process. Instead it proclaims the liberation of marriage.

We are deeply convinced, from our own experience as well as from observation of other good marriages, that true intimacy in the husband-wife relationship enhances rather than curtails the personal freedom of both partners. The very core of marital intimacy is full knowledge of each other resulting from the honesty and openness which characterize the relationship. And from that full knowledge springs complete trust and a sense of deep security and confidence in the invulnerability of the relationship. Under these conditions, and only under these conditions, can the partners give each other complete freedom.

Where we find possessiveness is in the marriage of limited involvement. Where life is not fully shared, where the other person is not fully known, there are always nagging uncertainties that rankle in the mind. These lead to a strong urge to make the relationship secure by tying down the partner in ways that challenge and curtail his personal freedom—by making demands, setting conditions, imposing limitations, expressing doubts, seeking assurances, and the like. The classical illustration of this is marital infidelity, which invariably develops in an atmosphere of deception and weaves a tangled web of further deception. The deception of each other by married partners is a frequently recurring theme in literature. Take deception out of marriage, and some novelists would have little left to write about!

The mutual involvement of married partners is not therefore a surrender of their personal freedom, but rather the way in which they choose to invest their freedom. Freedom is often mistakenly considered to be a process of keeping all possible options open as long as possible. But prolonged freedom to choose eventually destroys freedom to act because every action is a process of renouncing options to act otherwise. To insist that one will never become *involved* in a depth-relationship, which inevitably implies commitment, is in effect to cut oneself off from ever *experiencing* a depth-relationship.

Marriage as relationship-in-depth (a descriptive phrase we coined some years ago) therefore means maximum involvement. Yet it cannot mean *total* involvement. That would be impossible and undesirable. The point of maximum involvement must be discovered by each couple for themselves; but it can never reach the point at which the two circles completely overlap and become one.

This concept of marriage as a separateness in unity was expressed by the poet Khalil Gibran when he said, "Let there be spaces in your togetherness." [4] It was also referred to by the German poet Rilke, who wrote: "It is a question in marriage, to my feeling, not of creating a quick community of spirit by tearing down and destroying all boundaries, but rather a good marriage is that in which each appoints the other guardian of his solitude, and shows him this confidence, the greatest in his power to bestow. But, once the realization is accepted that even between the closest human beings infinite distances continue to exist, a wonderful living side by side can grow up." [5]

[4] Khalil Gibran, *The Prophet* (New York: Knopf, 1923), p. 15.
[5] Maria Rainer Rilke in an extract from an unidentified letter.

An amusing illustration can be used to describe the process by which married couples discover what for them constitutes maximum involvement. Imagine a group of porcupines settling down to sleep on a cold winter night. Being warm-blooded creatures, they huddle together in search of mutual warmth. But the point inevitably is reached when sharp quills prick tender flesh, and they recoil away from each other. In this fashion they shuffle sleepily back and forth, back and forth, until they find a point of equilibrium at which they derive the maximum possible amount of warmth from each other, consistent with not pricking each other!

The porcupines illustrate very well the process by which two married people achieve a close relationship. We could call it mutual adaptation. It means strengthening the affinities and resolving, as far as possible, the hostilities. It is a difficult art calling for skill and patience. But it can be learned; and those who learn it have in their hands the means to raise their involvement with each other as marriage partners to the highest level of which they as a couple are capable, without violating the sanctity of each other's personhood.

How is it done? In order to answer that question, we must explore the whole issue of conflict in marriage and how it is resolved. We shall do this in the next chapter.

CHAPTER 10

Marital Conflict—Friend in Disguise

We have seen that the quest for relationship-in-depth in marriage calls for higher levels of involvement between the couple and that increasing involvement sets up resistance on the part of the self—in both selves, to be precise. Carl Jung, the psychologist, expressed this by saying that marriage constitutes an invasion of the individual ego,[1] which it naturally resists at first until it can establish the necessary levels of tolerance.

Interestingly enough, something similar to this happens when a woman becomes pregnant. The fertilized ovum, after traveling slowly down the Fallopian tube, enters the womb and tries to attach itself to the inner lining so that it can draw nourishment from the mother's bloodstream for its continuing growth. At first the mother's body treats the developing new life as an invader and tries to fight it off; but if the invader manages to establish itself, all is well. The mother therefore, though unwittingly and unintentionally, begins by trying to push her baby away. Something similar to this happens in marriage as husband and wife seek to become more intimately involved in each other's lives. They throw up defenses against each other.

The moonstruck young couple, beginning their life together,

[1] Carl G. Jung, "Marriage as a Psychological Relationship" in H. Keyserling, ed. *The Book of Marriage*, pp. 352-55.

are appalled when conflict raises its ugly head. It seems to them that some sinister force from outside has invaded their relationship and is threatening to destroy their love. Not having been warned to expect this to happen, they panic and make every effort to evade and suppress it.

What they *should* be told is that conflict, far from being a hostile invader from outside, is in fact an integral part of a healthy marriage relationship. Indeed, it provides the essential information the couple need for the growth of their marriage; and if they suppress it they are actually denying themselves the chance to deepen their involvement.

This mechanism of evasion and suppression is what leads to the static concept of marriage which is widely accepted in our culture. It is often referred to as "settling down." In the courtship period, the couple play a very active game of advance and retreat, of exploration and negotiation, which is exciting and sometimes agonizing. But finally all this is apparently resolved in the decision to marry each other. In the traditional marriage, the husband now had corralled his bride and had no need to exert himself further to win her. So he returned to preoccupation with his business and his hobbies and no longer offered his beloved "flattery and flowers" to keep her in a good humor. For her the public ceremony, in which she occupied the center of the stage, was over, and she now capitulated to the humdrum routine of domesticity.

Along with the settling down concept went the belief that the couple must somehow try to keep alive the romantic atmosphere of their first love. The emergence of conflict was threatening and frightening because it seemed to destroy all chance of this. So they tended again to evade and suppress those ugly upsurges of hostility that darkened their days and led to late nights of futile and exhausting argument. They developed a stratagem of sealing off the sensitive areas by tacit agreement so as not to discuss them further. By thus avoiding conflict, they avoided pain. But they did so by limiting their mutual involvement and settling for a superficial relationship. The attempt to preserve the romantic love of the courtship days was unavailing, and slowly and imperceptibly they drifted apart. Before other people, they continued to act as though they were still very much in love, but behind the facade there was a relentlessly increasing sense of emptiness and futility.

This is a fair picture of large numbers of typical American marriages—except that more and more of these couples, in recent years, have no longer been prepared to tolerate their disillusionment and have dropped the pretenses and opted for divorce, thus boosting the figures for broken marriages to record highs.

What is fundamentally wrong in this situation is the failure to recognize that marital conflict, far from being a deadly enemy, is in fact a friend in disguise.

So let us look more closely at marital conflict. Marriage is the coming together of two unique and different individuals in order to share life with each other. Their differences are quite unavoidable. They have lived separate lives for perhaps twenty to twenty-five years, during which each has developed a set of individual tastes, preferences, habits, likes and dislikes, values and standards. It is totally unreasonable to suppose that two people, just because they are married to each other, should always want to do the same thing in the same way at the same time.

This doesn't happen even with identical twins. So the couple have differences of opinion and of choice, and these differences lead to disagreements. The couple may be quite willing to do the same thing in the same way, but at different times; or to do the same thing at the same time, but in different ways. How do they solve this problem? Either they must give up the idea altogether, and both feel frustrated and blame each other; or one will have to give up his particular wish and do it in the way, or at the time, the other wishes. People in love are able to do a good deal of giving up and giving in because love creates a generous mood. But sooner or later a situation develops in which neither is willing to accommodate the other because patience is exhausted, or enough ground has already been surrendered, or this time it is a matter of principle. So they are deadlocked, and now we have a conflict.

What exactly *is* marital conflict? It is a disagreement, a state of opposed wills, that has been *heated up by emotion*—anger, resentment, hurt feelings, anxiety. The emotion is caused by frustration because you want or need something and you can't get it.

What then is a disagreement which starts a conflict? It is a situation created by difference—two people with different wishes or objectives confront each other and are temporarily deadlocked.

Out of these simple elements we can make a picture of marital conflict. It is portrayed in diagram 5.

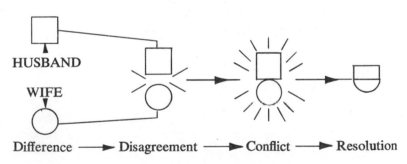

HUSBAND

WIFE

Difference ⟶ Disagreement ⟶ Conflict ⟶ Resolution

diagram 5
Conflict Resolution in Marriage

First we see the difference between husband and wife, illustrated by different shapes—a square and a circle. Next we see the difference in their wishes brought close together as a result of their desire for mutual involvement, which leads to a disagreement—each is asking the other to yield.

If they continue to confront each other in a state of disagreement, frustration is stirred in both and a state of emotional heat develops. This is conflict. They are moving into a clash of wills, a quarrel, a fight.

What they do next is critical. If they can't tolerate conflict, they will disengage and go back to where they started. The difference remains unresolved. The disagreement is recognized, but avoided in future, and the feelings of frustration suppressed. The attempt to become more deeply involved with each other, in that particular area of their relationship, is abandoned.

But suppose now that they recognize conflict as a friend in disguise and let their emotions heat up. And suppose that, instead of getting into a fight, they examine these hot emotions and try to understand their own and each other's feelings. It will then be possible to turn the conflict to good account by working together to resolve the original difference by some kind of adjustment or compromise. This is shown in the diagram as a figure that is a combination of the square and the circle.

Of course this is oversimplified. There are differences between husband and wife that can't be adjusted but must be tolerated. There are people who are good at settling disagreements with little or no conflict. There are situations in which compromise would be inappropriate and where one partner gracefully accepts the wishes of the other.

However, it should be clear enough that the difference between a bad marriage and a good marriage is based, more than on any other factor, on whether or not the couple learn the process of mutual adjustment that enables them to resolve their differences and to enter into a close and intimate interpersonal relationship. In other words, learning this process is the key that opens the door to the companionship marriage.

And it should be quite clear now why we have called marital conflict a friend in disguise. It is our conflicts that clearly identify for us the vital adjustments we *must* make if our marriages are to become the intimate, loving, trusting relationships we want them to be.

CHAPTER 11

The Concept of Marriage Enrichment

Millions of marriages soon stop growing and become frozen into levels of limited involvement far lower than those which the couples could achieve and want to achieve. This happens because they don't understand how to accept and resolve conflict, using it as a means of improving their relationship. It is perhaps the major tragedy of our society that we teach young people so many things, but do not teach them what Nelson Foote has aptly called "interpersonal competence." [1]

Why have we not done this? The answer is very simple. We have not taught it because, until relatively recently, we have not understood it. That doesn't mean that there have never been good marriages. There have been, probably in every age and in every culture. But good marriages in the sense in which we judge them today—companionship marriages, as we have chosen to call them in this book—have been rare indeed and have been achieved only in very unusual situations. Even so, the couples concerned have achieved relationship-in-depth without clearly understanding why. After all, only in the last half-century has marriage been seriously studied at all, so we haven't had very long to unravel its complexities.

[1] Nelson N. Foote and Leonard S. Cottrell, *Identity and Interpersonal Competence* (Chicago: University of Chicago Press, 1955).

At this point it will be worthwhile to take a brief look at the way in which our marriage patterns have evolved over a period of a century or so. There are three stages which we can clearly distinguish, and we will call our little game "Where to Draw the Line." It is all summed up in diagram 6.

(1) Conflict-excluding   (2) Conflict-avoiding   (3) Conflict-resolving

diagram 6
Three Patterns of Marriage

The first picture shows the traditional marriage, which reflects the patriarchal family pattern. It is pretty clear where the line is drawn in this one. Above it is the husband, in the position of authority and power, in control of the situation, and making all the important decisions. Below the line is the wife, submissive and obedient. Conflict is simply excluded by making marriage a one-vote system. In the past, when the stability of the family was considered to be essential for social and cultural survival, this system guaranteed it. Differences and disagreements were simply suppressed. Religion and law combined to keep the man in power and the woman subservient to him.

The second picture shows what has happened as a result of the revolt against the traditional marriage. Husband and wife have been placed side by side as equal partners. In theory this is just and good; but unfortunately, it has failed to work in practice. Instead of cooperating sweetly and smoothly, husband and wife have both asserted themselves, and their differences have created an endless series of disagreements. The two-vote system involves a very awkward complication. What happens when they vote on opposite sides?

These disagreements have produced severe conflicts which have been painful and frustrating. With no understanding of how to resolve conflict, the couples concerned have taken the only course open to them—to put distance between them. Remember what we said about the field a mile square, where the couple could get out of shouting distance of each other?

However, these couples couldn't put *spatial* distance between them because they had to go on sleeping together in that 150 square feet of bedroom. So instead they put *psychological* distance between them. They stopped communicating and tuned each other out. They drew the line vertically between them, in the form of thick layers of verbal and emotional insulation. They learned to be physically near each other, but in spirit far separated. This enabled them to avoid the conflicts they so much dreaded and to make their relationship so superficial that they scaled it down to something like minimum involvement. Millions of American marriages are like this. It represents the standard pattern with which marriage counselors are confronted every day.

The third picture shows the liberated companionship marriage. The couple are side by side, just as in the second picture. Indeed, the two pictures may at first glance look deceptively alike. But there are two important differences between them. Look where the line has been drawn in this picture—as a solid, secure base beneath the feet of both. And notice that their hands are joined—they are in close, warm physical and emotional contact with each other.

Finally, notice how the transition from one pattern to the next takes place. In the first shift, husband and wife change positions as the result of a social revolution which insists on equality of the sexes. But to their disappointment this doesn't fulfill their expectations that it will bring greater happiness. There is no way back to where they were before, even if they wanted to take it. The only solution, as the dividing barrier grows greater and greater, is to get out of the marriage altogether.

In the second shift, husband and wife don't change positions. So no further social revolution can bring this about. The transition from the second pattern to the third can be made *only by the couple themselves* and only by facing and resolving their conflicts. They must reach out to each other and take hold of each other's hands. They must get back into real communication. Then they must begin the long, difficult process of dismantling the barrier they have built up between them; and they must instead build a solid foundation under their feet.

More and more couples are learning to do this today. They are the couples who are beginning to understand at last what modern marriage is all about. Many of them are getting help from people like family life educators and marriage counselors. Others are beginning to read and think and talk together about the widespread disillusionment with which marriage is being viewed today; and they are coming up with some positive answers. These couples are a minority. But they are a vanguard of pioneers pointing the way for millions of others to follow. They are part of what we are now beginning to call the marriage enrichment movement.

We don't know who coined the term "marriage enrichment." We used it in the title of one of our books which was published back in 1952, but we were not at that time consciously inventing new terminology. Whether it is a good term or not is beside the point. It is undoubtedly the term many people are seizing upon to describe what they want. They are tired of a dull, empty, routinized married life. Yet they don't want to end their marriages. In that situation, the idea of being able to enrich them surely is attractive!

So we are offering them enrichment. We don't mean putting into marriage something new from outside, some additive that will make it sparkle, as manufacturers enrich bread or cereal or motor oil. We mean the opposite of that—drawing out potentialities in the marriage that are already there, unrealized and undeveloped. We sometimes quote the remark, attributed to Albert Einstein, that most of us go through life without using more than about 10 percent of our intellectual potential, suggesting that most of us likewise go through married life with a mere fraction of our capacity for love and companionship either realized or expressed.

The enrichment concept also includes growth. We have no interest in the static marriage. We believe that a marriage is a living entity, unique as the persons who share it are unique, and capable of change and development as they change and develop. We believe that most people have a latent capacity, and a desperate need, to give and receive love. Often this capacity has been inhibited and restrained in our culture; yet it can stir and awake and come alive when the right conditions are created. And we believe we are beginning to discover how those conditions *can* be created. The evidence that is unfolding is very impressive. Once a couple have registered the decision that they want their marriage to grow, they have taken the first decisive step. Since the greatest hindrance to marital growth is the inability of most couples to resolve conflict positively and creatively, it is at this point that the process of marriage enrichment must begin.

The next step is for them to open up fully the channels of communication between them that have long been closed and sealed. This is a painful process, and they usually need encouragement, help, and support. The inevitable result of being honest with each other is of course that old, buried, unresolved conflicts will be reactivated. But if they now fully understand what they are doing and what the rewards are likely to be, they find themselves able to do what they never did before— to handle conflict constructively, making real progress. This brings great encouragement and helps them to continue with the work of pulling down the barriers. If they continue to need help and support, it should be available to them. Finally they reach a point at which they have registered sufficient gains to know that it would be folly not to go on and realize the further potential which their relationship holds out to them. At that point they have become convinced believers in marriage enrichment, and a new life has opened up for them.

CHAPTER 12

Communication—The Master Key

"I can't hear you, darling!"

The speaker could be an anxious wife who was beginning to grow deaf or an agitated husband driving through a tumult of traffic while his wife was trying to tell him where to turn.

At a deeper level, however, this statement takes us near to the heart of all marriage failures. Sooner or later, all attempts on the part of husbands and wives to resolve their conflicts and to enrich their relationships confront them with the vital issue of communication. As we have sometimes expressed it, relationship-in-depth can only be achieved and can only be sustained, through communication-in-depth.

A marriage can be likened to a large house with many rooms to which a couple fall heir on their wedding day. Their hope is to use and enjoy these rooms, as we do the rooms in a comfortable home, so that they will serve the many activities that make up their shared life. But in many marriages, doors are found to be locked—they represent areas in the relationship which the couple are unable to explore together. Attempts to open these doors lead to failure and frustration. The right key cannot be found. So the couple resign themselves to living together in only a few rooms that can be opened easily, leaving the rest of the house, with all its promising possibilities, unexplored and unused. This represents the kind of superficial marriage which we have already discussed.

There is, however, a master key that will open every door. It is not easy to find. Or, more correctly, it has to be forged by the couple together, and this can be very difficult. It is the great art of effective marital communication.

Human communication is a very complex subject. It has been extensively studied and constitutes a specialized part of the field of behavioral science. Until recently, most of the written material in this field has been highly technical, and therefore not available to most people. This is unfortunate in the extreme because ordinary men and women need this information very much. It would not be an exaggeration to say that most of the problems that arise in the world do so because people can't get along harmoniously with one an other, and these are fundamentally problems of communication. This is particularly true of marriage problems.

Fortunately, all this is now being realized, and many efforts are being made to get our knowledge about human communication down to the level at which it can be of practical use. A good example is the system of transactional analysis developed by Eric Berne,[1] which has recently been enjoying very wide popularity. Another example is the cultivation of creative listening training experiences. There are now also some projects being developed to help couples to improve marital communication. One that has impressed us is the Minnesota Couple Communication Program (MCCP)[2] developed by Sherod Miller and his associates.

We believe that the training of couples in effective marital communication should be a basic part of all marriage enrichment programs, and also of all marriage preparation programs.

[1] Eric Berne, *Transactional Analysis in Psychotherapy* (New York: Grove Press, 1961). A popularized version appears in the bestseller by Thomas A. Harris, *I'm OK, You're OK* (New York: Harper & Row, 1967).
[2] Minnesota Couple Communication Program, 2001 Riverside Avenue, Minneapolis, Minn. 55404.

It is already an integral part of most competent marriage counseling.

What would such training involve? It would begin by teaching couples to get their messages across to one another so that there was no misunderstanding. The misinterpretation by one partner of what the other is trying to say is a frequent form of breakdown in marital communication. The couple can learn to avoid it by practicing a process of feedback and confirmation. Here is an example:

Husband: "I felt jealous last night when Jack Jones kissed you at the party."

Wife: "I'm not surprised. I know you don't like him. But what could I do? I couldn't push him away."

Husband: "I know. I'm not blaming you. I just couldn't help my feelings."

This *could* have been an explosive situation. The wife could have taken her husband's statement as an accusation. She might then have felt angry, defended herself, and attacked her husband for distrusting her. But she realized that he was honestly sharing how he had felt, and she said so clearly in her response. He then confirmed the fact that she had understood him and assured her that he had no ill feeling toward her. Thus a potential crisis was averted.

Another aspect of training is to teach couples to recognize the different levels at which husbands and wives communicate. The MCCP breaks these down into four *styles*.

Husband: "Maybe I should go and fix Bonny's dollhouse. It needs some repairs."

Wife: "That's a good idea. She likes playing with it, but it's not much good in its present condition."

This is style I, which is simply friendly, sociable conversation—the kind of communication that goes on in the average home most of the time.

A few minutes later, the husband returns.

Husband: "I can't find the hammer. Have you seen it?"

100

Wife: "Oh, I had it today. Let's see. Oh yes, I left it on the kitchen counter."

Husband: "You did, did you? Why can't you put things back where they belong when you're through with them?"

This is style II. The husband is irritated, and he is making a complaint. He is putting his wife down. This is unfortunately a rather common pattern of communication in marriage.

The wife now has two options. She can react in the same spirit, also using style II.

Wife: "Don't be so mean. If you want to know, I was just too busy cooking your dinner!"

This is likely to reinforce the husband's irritation and bring forth from him another style II statement. They could then drift into a quarrel which might spoil their evening.

The wife could however use her other option.

Wife: "I'm sorry, dear. Just at that point the soup boiled over, and I forgot about it."

Husband: "OK. But you should have said so in the first place."

This could end the conversation. But the wife might follow it up by inviting further discussion.

Wife: "Maybe I should. But John, you don't give me the benefit of the doubt, do you? I wish we didn't flare up so easily. Couldn't we be a bit more tolerant toward each other?"

Husband: "Well, I guess it would be better if we could. Fighting doesn't do us any good."

The wife has now moved to style III, in spite of her husband's not very helpful rejoinder. And the husband has also responded in style III. Neither is now scaling down the other. Instead, they are showing their willingness to look at the problem and acknowledging that they don't really approve of the negative communication pattern into which they very easily tend to drift.

However, they are not likely to do anything about it. They have looked at the problem, but only tentatively. Neither has taken a really decisive step toward changing it. That requires style IV. The wife continues:

Wife: "John, I'd like to talk more about this. Why don't you sit down a minute. This is more important to us than Bonny's dollhouse. I know I often irritate you by my forgetfulness, and I don't like myself for it. I sometimes lie awake at night and wonder how I can be a better wife to you. I want to make you happy, John, I really do. Will you help me to understand you better, so that I don't irritate you so often?"

This is the form of marital communication that leads to action. It is a here-and-now desire for change. It involves letting down defenses and making yourself vulnerable, while doing nothing to put the other partner on the defensive, so that it constitutes an invitation to him also to let down his defenses and make himself vulnerable. He may not respond, in which case there is nothing else that can be done at this present time. But if he does respond, now or later, the way is open to work together at the problem, and to make a genuine cooperative effort to resolve it.

Using style IV doesn't come naturally because in our general social life in the community we are taught to be on our guard, to hide our deeper feelings, to protect ourselves, to stand up for our rights. Many couples carry these patterns over into marriage, and it is little wonder that they never achieve real intimacy or companionship. Yet any couple can be taught to recognize the four styles, to try them out with each other, and to learn to use them in the appropriate settings. The MCCP course, which covers much more than the four styles, requires only four evenings of three hours each, spaced out at weekly intervals, with homework in between. It is taken by a group of six to eight couples together. In that short period many couples report that their relationship is greatly improved.

These are merely illustrations. The subject is a vast one, and as yet very little understood outside a small circle of specialists. Yet the examples we have given, which could be extensively multiplied, surely illustrate the fact that we have here a vast untapped resource of knowledge and skill which could shift the balance in many a marriage from constant irritation and misery to growth and fulfillment.

Since we cannot pursue this matter further (that would require another book) let us at least indicate some of the aspects of marital communication which couples should be helped to understand.

1. Because marriage is a relationship of shared intimacy, it requires a level of honesty between the partners that goes much deeper than conventional social relationships. People cannot truly share life without knowing each other, and they cannot know each other unless their thoughts are open to each other to a degree that happens in few other human relationships. To be secretive or reserved or defensive toward each other in marriage is inevitably to condemn the relationship to superficiality.

2. In particular, this means honesty about *feelings*. Love between man and woman begins as a rapturous positive feeling, but the shared life awakens in both partners, inevitably, negative emotions as well. These need not be deplored—anger is a healthy emotion in the right place. However, in marriage it can be dangerous. Yet to suppress it may do more harm than to express it. The best solution is for a couple to learn to communicate their anger honestly to each other, recognize it as a barrier to their happiness, and cooperate in resolving it.

3. In order to communicate effectively a husband or wife must achieve as much self-awareness as possible. It is baffling not to understand one's actions or emotions. Some people need counseling about this, and such personal counseling may help them to function better as marriage partners. It is our view, however, that this counseling toward self-awareness can often be facilitated if the marriage partner is also involved.

103

Growing in self-awareness and in the capacity to relate to the partner are processes that complement and reinforce one another—a fact often ignored by some therapists.

4. Distorted perception of each other is often a barrier to effective marital communication. As Oliver Wendell Holmes pointed out,[3] there are three Johns—the real John, known only to his Maker, John's ideal John, and Mary's ideal John. There are likewise three Marys. All of these six people are involved together in any marriage, and in a really meaningful relationship they must all have some acquaintance with each other. If this sounds discouraging, it need not be. Plenty of honest and open communication will not only make the distinctions between the three Johns and the three Marys clear, it will do something better. It will help to merge the three into one, which is another way of saying that it will be a maturing process for both John and Mary.

5. One reason why people don't hear each other is because they tune one another out. Communication experts tell us that the average person receives about sixteen hundred messages daily, but acts only on about twelve of them. So we obviously have a well-developed capacity to block out what we don't want to hear! In many marriages communication is so superficial and so little is known by each about the real interests of the other that a great deal of conversation virtually falls on deaf ears. This leads to chronic boredom, which is a deadly condition when it afflicts a marriage. Couples who practice honest sharing of their thoughts and feelings are able to focus their communication on matters that are of genuine interest to each other, and therefore continue to enjoy each other's company.

6. In this discussion we have been considering only what is called *verbal* communication—the use of words to convey messages and express feelings. But there was plenty of com-

---

[3] Oliver Wendell Holmes, *The Autocrat of the Breakfast-Table* (New York: Hill & Wang, 1957), chapter 3.

munication before the development of language, and we still do a lot of our communicating through body postures, movements, and gestures. Sometimes a person will say one thing verbally, but something quite different nonverbally; and it is very helpful if marriage partners can be aware of this, because the nonverbal message may well be the real one. An increasing interest in "body language" and "sensory awareness" has been developing lately, and some understanding of this should be part of any training in couple communication.

This chapter has focused attention on a vitally important area of interpersonal relationship in marriage. If it has done nothing else it may have helped to make us aware of how much we all need to learn about marital communication and how learning about it can contribute both to the growth of the partners and to their increased enjoyment of one another. It is indeed the master key.

CHAPTER 13

Find Your Place on the Marriage Chart

Those readers who are themselves married may, during our discussion, have been thinking of their own relationship. The concept of marriage enrichment, stressing as it does the potential for growth, encourages us to ask ourselves where we personally stand.

We sometimes use a series of simple statements to help husbands and wives to assess their marriages. Here they are:

1. I believe our marriage has developed very well. I am deeply satisfied with it and am hopeful that it will continue to grow.

2. I would say we have a good marriage, and I am on the whole satisfied. However, there are a few aspects of it that could be improved to make our relationship better still.

3. Our marriage is a stable one and certainly not in any danger. Yet I am aware that, in terms of what I expected and hoped for, our relationship leaves a good deal to be desired.

4. I must admit that our marriage has been deeply disappointing to me, and we are suffering a lot of unhappiness as a result. I wish something could be done about it.

5. Our marriage has been a failure, and I really see no hope that it can ever be any good. I would like to get out of it as soon as possible.

These statements cover a wide range. If each partner tries

to decide which statement most nearly represents the marriage as it is right now, the two will not necessarily agree. Nor will either of them necessarily feel the same way about it today as they did yesterday, or as they will tomorrow. All the same, trying to make an honest assessment can often help to clear the air. And any attempt to face the realities of the situation is better than evading the issue and doing nothing. Studies have shown that the average American marriage, as perceived by husbands and wives, grows progressively less satisfactory as the years pass. A marriage that is allowed to drift, therefore, is more likely to drift downward than upward.

As a further aid to married couples, and to those who try to help them, we have designed a "marriage chart" which includes some of the concepts which we have been discussing in this book. It is outlined in diagram 7.

The horizontal dimension represents the length of time the couple have been married—up to forty years. The vertical line shows the ups and downs of marriage. The middle point would represent a marriage that is acceptable to the couple— neither good nor bad, but tolerable. Above the line marriages get better and better until they reach the point of maximum potential—the peak of satisfaction for both partners. Below the line marriages get worse and worse until they reach the point of complete breakdown, represented by separation or divorce.

We have drawn two diagonal lines to represent imaginary marriages, both starting at the middle line. The one sloping upward represents continual growth during the forty years, reaching its maximum potential. The downward-sloping one represents steady degeneration over the same period, ending finally in breakdown.

These sloping lines, and the middle line, divide the chart into four triangular areas. Moving clockwise, the first represents the enriched marriage, the second the stable superficial marriage, the third the unstable superficial marriage, and the

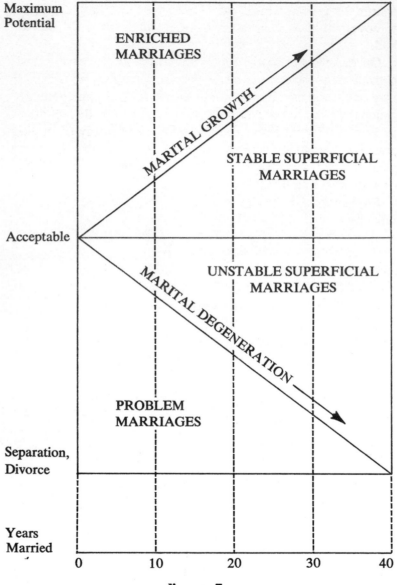

diagram 7
THE MARRIAGE CHART

fourth the problem marriage. These are the terms we choose to cover the full range of marriages, from very good to very bad.

On this chart it is possible for any husband or wife to sketch a graph of his or her marriage. Of course there is no objective way of measuring this. How good or how bad your marriage is depends, in the last resort, on how you personally feel about it. But it is useful to have some quite specific way of putting your feelings about your marriage on a chart and comparing what has actually happened with what could have happened or with what might still happen.

Every marriage that has ever existed could be shown on this chart. You might like to try it with yours. All you have to do is to consider, for each year you have been married, how good, or bad, your marriage was in that particular year: choose a spot on the chart that you consider represents this and make a small cross at that spot. Then join all the crosses together, and you get a graph showing your marriage.

Consider some possibilities. Although it would be very unlikely, a marriage could theoretically reach its full potential soon after it began, and stay there all through the forty years. Most really good marriages grow more gradually than that, but all of them would be in the "enriched marriages" triangle for all or most of the years. The imaginary marriage we have sketched in would represent the lower limit of this area—a marriage that started as just acceptable and grew steadily until it reached its full potential.

If we now consider the "stable superficial" triangle, this would include all marriages from the one we have just described, down to one that started as barely acceptable and stayed that way for the whole forty years, growing no better and no worse. Between these extremes there would be marriages that stayed at the acceptable level for some years and then took an upward turn, marriages that started growing in a promising way but then dropped down to the level of being little more than acceptable, and marriages that wavered up and down, from year to year, within these limits.

All the marriages in this triangle would be stable, in the sense that there was never any serious threat that they would break down. But they would be superficial in the sense that they would not become relationships of any depth or achieve a great deal of mutual involvement—except for some of them in the later years. There are plenty of marriages in this category, and many of the couples may be quite satisfied with a superficial relationship until they either begin to see possibilities of enrichment which they had not considered seriously before or until they drop below the "acceptable" level and become unstable.

In the third triangle we find the "unstable superficial" marriages. In these marriages the relationship is so superficial that misunderstandings, disagreements, and conflicts easily develop, and the relationship goes through periodical episodes of trouble. The trouble may never be very serious, although it is disturbing. In that event the marriage will never fall far below the "acceptable" line. But in other cases the marriage may be so unstable that it will slip down to the point of degeneration and finally end in breakdown.

In the final triangle are the "problem" marriages. These are relationships that are so superficial and so unstable, that they are in real danger of dropping to the breakdown point. This may take a long period of gradual degeneration, like the imaginary marriage represented by the downward-sloping line. It is possible, however, for a marriage starting at the "acceptable" line to drop down very sharply to the point at which it quickly ends in separation or divorce.

The graph representing any particular marriage need not be confined to one of these triangles. It could sprawl across all of them, though this is not likely. There have been marriages that fell seriously into the problem area and yet, through the determined efforts of the couple and with good counseling help, managed to climb in the end into the stable, or even into the enriched, area. There may even be marriages that experience a period of enrichment and yet fall to lower levels, though we think this is highly improbable. In general, we think that once a married couple achieve relationship-in-depth, the chances that they will fall down to the superficial or the problem area are quite remote.

The chart is not intended to represent numbers of marriages in the various areas, although the triangles are all of equal size. Nor is it intended to represent any average trends or norms. As we have already indicated, the average American marriage slowly falls to lower levels of satisfaction as the years pass. This is unfortunate, and our argument in this book is that it need not be so. The answer lies in awakening the large number of couples in the triangles representing superficial marriages, both stable and unstable, both to their danger and to the unrecognized possibilities of growth and enrichment that are open to them.

One point should be very clearly understood. The enriched marriage didn't get to be that way by accident or good fortune. It is always, as we understand it, the result of deliberate, enlightened effort on the part of both partners working together. The development of a really good marriage is not a natural process. It is an achievement.

If an honest appraisal of your marriage suggests that it is somewhere in the second, third, or even fourth triangles, you may want to consider how you can change it into a true companionship marriage. This is not an easy task, especially for marriages in the fourth triangle. But many couples have achieved it, and many more could do so. In the chapters that follow, we shall try to tell you how this can be done.

PART III

Resources for Marriage Enrichment

CHAPTER 14

The Limits of Individual Effort

If we now have a much clearer understanding of why marriages fail and know that many couples could achieve the kind of relationship they really want and need, why not just tell them and let them get on with the job?

How wonderful it would be if that were possible! But it isn't. We find this hard to believe. We stubbornly resist such a negative judgment. Since the time of the ancient Greek philosophers, and probably before that, we have persisted with almost unbelievable optimism in clinging to the idea that since man is a rational being, he can direct his life by the simple process of putting into action what he knows intellectually to be sensible and right. Yet all the time we are surrounded by masses of incontrovertible evidence that this is not true.

We do not say that knowledge is not very important and highly valuable. Scientific knowledge has totally transformed our lives in the past half century. But it has done so mainly by changing our environment—not by changing us. The extent to which our behavior is really changed by knowledge is very small indeed. What decides our behavior is not what we know, but what we want and need; not information, but our emotions and our habit patterns.

Even when we think knowledge is changing us, in most cases it really isn't. If you discover a quicker way to drive to work, you will probably change your route—but only if one of your basic aims in life is not to spend any longer than necessary on the way to work. Even then you may soon go back to the longer route if you decide that you prefer the scenery or that it lessens your chances of being involved in an accident. In other words, we only act on knowledge if the course of action it suggests is in accordance with what we want and what we are willing to do. Otherwise, we discard it and go our own way.

The situation is even worse than that. Freud showed us clearly that we actually get ourselves into predicaments that result in the very opposite of what we want and need because we are driven by unconscious, immature desires which, in our lives here and now, don't make sense at all. And even when we discover new ways of behaving that are much better for us and for everyone else concerned, we can never be sure that deeply engrained habits won't take over and pull us back to where we started.

In other words, the idea that we respond in changed behavior to new concepts of behavior which we learn about, as a ship responds to the helmsman when the order is given to change course, is a complete illusion. And what we mean by saying this is that if you have read carefully what we have written so far about how marriages can be enriched, you will probably do nothing about it. You will possibly imagine your marriage better and happier and even get excited about the idea. But it will end up as a pleasant, passive fantasy. You might even mention the idea to your spouse, who will probably be skeptical or indifferent. Even if your spouse should get interested in the idea and also read the book, there are still a thousand ways in which the project could get stalled. All of us have dreamed dreams about how we could make our lives better and happier, and most of them have turned out to be no more than pipe dreams.

So we must say at the outset, very firmly, that the self-help way to marriage enrichment, like the self-help way to losing weight or gaining self-confidence, offers little hope for most of us. It would be easy for us to write out for you a series of steps that you could take to improve your marital communication, to resolve your marital conflicts, or to develop positive interaction. It has already been done. There are plenty of excellent books available on how to succeed in marriage. There are even records and cassettes which you can play over together at home. Unfortunately we have met very few couples who testify that the use of these materials improved their relationship. In most cases, the books have gone back to the shelves, the records to the cabinet, and the marriage has continued just as before.

We have become deeply convinced that the real agents of change in our lives are *other people with whom we become involved.* Just as the achievement of a truly satisfying marriage comes from the deepening of mutual involvement between the partners, so the motivation to work at enriching a marriage comes from involvement with people who can guide and support our efforts (like marriage counselors) and people who can join with us in the same kind of endeavor (like other couples in a group). Reading about marriage enrichment or hearing about it can be a very significant first step in giving us the idea, in telling us what is possible. But nothing significant is going to happen for most of us until we take the decisive step of linking up with other people who can work with us and hold us to achieve our purpose. If you disagree with us, by all means try the self-help route. We shall be delighted if you can prove us wrong. But if we prove to be right, we hope you will then consider the alternative procedure which we recommend.

Because of the limits of isolated individual effort, we have undertaken in this book to place the emphasis on the steps a couple can take to become involved with others—by seeking the help of a professional person, by participating in a growth group experience for married couples, or, best of all, by joining a new national Association of Couples for Marriage Enrichment which we have set up and which will be described in the final chapter.

If what we have said here is discouraging, it is also realistic. We confidently believe that large numbers of couples really can achieve much better marriages than they have. But this will not happen as a result of reading about it, hearing about it, or even thinking about it. It will happen only when they commit themselves to *action,* to the making of ventures, to the inevitable hazards of new experiences, and when they join with others who are pursuing the same goal. Then, we promise you, things *will* happen!

CHAPTER 15

What Counseling Can Offer

We have been involved in the development of marriage counseling during the major part of our professional lives. This has been one of our major preoccupations. We knew that many married couples desperately needed help, and we set out to provide that help.

Marriage counseling has come a long way in that time. The first book to appear on the subject, published in 1948,[1] is now a museum specimen. We shudder to think of how little we knew when we dealt with our first cases. But nobody else at that time knew any more, so we simply did our best. It was little more than a process of giving advice. We tried to figure out what we would do if we were in the same trouble and offered our opinion for what it was worth. Our opinion was probably worth a lot less than the fact that we gave those unhappy couples a sympathetic hearing.

We soon tried to improve on these simple techniques. Since the professional approach to personal difficulties at that time was psychoanalysis, we dug deeply into psychology and tried to put our knowledge to use. Since psychoanalysts never saw

---

[1] David Mace, *Marriage Counseling* (London: Churchill, 1948). It was published in England only a few months before the first American book on the subject by John Cuber.

two people together, we adopted at first the same principle. We saw husband and wife separately and tried to find out what could be wrong with their personalities, arguing that there must be something wrong if they couldn't succeed in an enterprise as natural as married life. We found plenty that was wrong in most cases, but we were not conspicuously successful in doing anything about it. However, we were friendly, compassionate, and concerned, and that seemed to help. We had our successes as well as our failures.

In time, studies of marriage emphasized that husband and wife lived in a small social system and that their interactions to each other could make all the difference between success and failure. This suggested that it might be more sensible to see them together and actually observe those interactions. So we started to do what is called conjoint counseling, and found we were making headway, although we still recognized the need to do some of the counseling with husband or wife alone.

This led to a shift in our basic emphasis, which was helped along by the growing interest in behavior modification. When we followed the psychoanalytic model, we took the view that changing attitudes through insight would lead to the necessary changes in behavior. We now discovered that changing behavior could quickly change attitudes and that behavior *could* be changed by getting the couple to try out, in joint interviews and also at home, new ways of interacting with one another. So we began to develop the technique of getting our couples to do "homework" between interviews—a procedure very successfully used by Masters and Johnson in the treatment of sexual inadequacy.[2] We also, following Masters and Johnson, experimented with co-counselors working with the couple as a "foursome."

These trends led to subtle but important changes in the marriage counselor's concept of his task. At first he saw him-

[2] William H. Masters and Virginia E. Johnson, *Human Sexual Inadequacy* (Boston: Little, Brown & Co., 1970).

self in an authoritative role. He listened to what the husband and wife told him. He asked many questions and gathered information. He made a diagnosis. Then he tried to get the couple to see the situation as he saw it, which was supposed to be enough to put them on the right track.

Lately the counselor has been shifting his ground to that of a consultant. He is less and less willing to "take over" and let the couple become dependent on him. He sees the problem as squarely theirs, and they alone can solve it. They have to decide what they want in their marriage that isn't there. And they have to want it enough to work hard, both of them, to get it. Under these conditions, the counselor will give them guidance, help, and support. But it must be quite clearly understood who is doing the work. *They* are.

Marriage counselors who have moved into this role are generally well satisfied with it. They get better results and feel better about what they do. Without altogether realizing it, they are really getting into marriage enrichment. The problem focus is beginning to recede into the background. One highly experienced counselor, Howard Clinebell, even says that he doesn't care to call his sessions with couples "counseling" any more. He prefers to use the term "training." He is teaching couples new methods of interacting with each other which will enable them to attain in their relationships the goal they have already agreed upon. The couples, he reports, also like the idea that they are being trained much better than that of being counseled.

What is happening here? We interpret it as a shift in focus from a remedial to a preventive approach, from an emphasis on "How can we save our marriage?" to "How can we make our marriage grow?"

Individual marriage counselors are of many persuasions and from many disciplines, and they may be found using any or all of the approaches we have described. But our opinion, as well as our hope and expectation, is that the trend in the future will be in the direction we have indicated.

There are of course deeply disturbed people who inevitably land themselves in deeply disturbed marriages. There are no shortcuts for these people, who need a great deal of therapy of a supportive kind. This can very well be marital and family therapy—indeed, there is a decided trend toward the view that it was in a poor family setting that most of these people suffered personality damage and that in an improved family setting lies their best opportunity of being healed. But for every person thus deeply disoriented there are many who are in marriage difficulties simply because they need to learn the skills in interpersonal relationships which they were never taught. Such people do not need therapy in any technical sense of the word—they need training in the art of being married, and once convinced of this they make apt pupils and learn quickly.

We hope the time will soon come when marriage counselors will be identified more clearly in the role of trainers and facilitators for married couples who need to learn the skills necessary for effective conflict resolution so that they can develop deep and satisfying interpersonal involvement. A couple came to us recently and said simply, "Our marriage isn't breaking up. We are quite sure we want to stay married. But we have both decided that we want our next twenty years together to be a whole lot better than our last twenty years have been." That was a plain, straightforward request for marriage enrichment on an individual couple basis, and it is our view that most marriage counselors would warmly welcome such an approach.

The exasperating difficulty faced by marriage counselors from the beginning has been that couples are hesitant to admit they need help until the situation is desperate. Then, in deep distress, they come to the counselor and expect him to work miracles. By this time, in many instances, the relationship has been severely damaged, and the motivation of husband and wife to work on it has been almost exhausted. Little can be done to help marriages in this advanced state of disintegration. They generally break up in the end, and the skill of the counselor may be questioned because he couldn't prevent this; very much as the reputation of a surgeon might soon suffer if most of his patients came to him suffering from inoperable cancers.

What is so regrettable is that if these same couples had understood the need for training in marital adjustment and had come to the same counselor years earlier, he could in many instances have started them together on the right road so that they would have been spared marital suffering and misery altogether.

The best policy of all would be to encourage couples preparing for marriage to start their training at that point. We are not speaking here of the kind of didactic "preparation for marriage" offered through reading books, hearing lectures, or receiving "instruction." Much of this has been attempted by the most sincere and well-meaning persons, but we have to express in all honesty our opinion that this is too superficial to achieve our purpose. A more intensive kind of preparation, however, can be offered that does provide training in interpersonal interaction, and that can be followed up by a system of check-ups which can do a great deal to get any reasonably well-matched couple off to a good start.

This kind of positive, preventive work could be very effectively done by well-qualified marriage counselors. Some of them have tried to develop it, but have been disappointed by the poor response from couples moving into marriage. We are of the opinion that a determined campaign to provide this service on a competent basis and to explain its obvious value to young people considering marriage would in time change all this. Youth today are no longer in a mood to believe the sentimental romantic nonsense about marriage that was sold to the previous generation. They know very well, from what is happening around them, the hazards that beset those who marry, and the risks of failure. Offer them a sound, convincing service which will train them to achieve effective, healthy, growing marriage relationships, and our guess is that they will gladly make use of it.

Marriage counseling, at first regarded with suspicion and mistrust, is now an accepted and established profession. There are still some quacks around, but those who have met the professional standards of bodies like the American Association of Marriage and Family Counselors[3] or of the Family Service Association of America[4] can be trusted to know what they are doing. If more and more of these counselors could be switched from the difficult and often discouraging task of striving to make a little hard-won progress with chronic cases and set to work to train younger and more teachable couples who want to learn how to achieve companionship marriages that really work, those depressing divorce figures might stop climbing higher and higher and begin at last to come down again.

[3] American Association of Marriage and Family Counselors, 225 Yale Avenue, Claremont, Calif. 91711.
[4] Family Service Association of America, 44 East 23 Street, New York, N.Y. 10001.

CHAPTER 16

The Stimulus of Group Interaction

Bethel is the name of a small town (population 950), near the western border of Maine. In the year 1947, a group meeting took place there that was to make history. It proved to be the first of a long series of similar group meetings that came to be known by many names—training labs, sensitivity training groups, encounter groups, growth groups, to name only a few of them. The basic ideas behind these groups came from social psychologist Kurt Lewin. The concept was not that of group therapy, which was already well established. These were short-term group experiences that promised to help ordinary people to understand themselves better, to change their behavior toward others, and generally to improve their skills in managing human relationships.

Participation in these group experiences became very popular, and millions of people were ultimately involved, here in the United States and in other countries. Controversy raged around the movement, and it was rumored that incompetent leadership in some of the groups was causing serious damage to sensitive and unstable persons. This complaint proved to be well founded—many participants afterwards required psychiatric treatment, and some needed to be hospitalized. On the other hand, careful follow-up studies[1] showed that a size-

[1] A careful study of eighteen encounter groups by Morton A. Lieberman of the University of Chicago found that more than one-third of the participants benefited, but 20 percent were "psychiatric casualties."

able proportion of participants derived great and lasting benefit.

The first wave of popular enthusiasm for these group experiences has now died down. Much has been learned that provides us with new methods of helping men and women to find themselves and their proper place in our complex modern society. The extreme procedures that created sensational publicity have now been largely eradicated, and growth groups of many kinds, under responsible supervision and leadership, are an accepted part of our culture today.

These groups were set up to provide experiences for individuals. Some of them welcomed married couples, but tended to find it confusing to include two people with an existing special relationship in what was otherwise a group of separate persons. When marital conflict erupted, as it sometimes did, this seemed to upset the normal group process. Some experienced group leaders began to discourage married couples from attending together.

In time, however, experiments began to be made with groups set up exclusively for married couples. Some of these were little more than study groups with the marriage relationship as the central topic. Others tried out some of the procedures used in other types of growth groups, with varied results.

All serious investigators tend to agree, however, that married couples get along very well together in groups and are often very helpful to each other. It began to become clear that groups of married couples are quite different, in some important respects, from groups of individuals. As one experienced leader put it, this was "a group of subgroups," and each subgroup was an existing social unit with a shared past and the prospect of a continuing shared future. The subgroups also interact with a comfortable feeling that they are all sharing a common experience, whereas the average group of separate individuals will be much more aware of wide differences.

The couples, as they gain in mutual confidence and trust, tend to incorporate the others into their own relationship so that a strong sense of being a large family often emerges. When a married couple lead the group (a highly desirable arrangement in our opinion), these become the adopted parents and tend to be treated as models.

Our own experience of leading groups of married couples began in 1962, when the growth groups were less well known. In the following years we experimented widely with different methods and cautiously tried out procedures that had proved successful in other types of group experience.

We soon became aware of a peculiar feature of groups of married couples. So long as we discussed marriage in general terms, all went well. But whenever we invited couples to tell other couples what was happening in their own marriages, we encountered resistance; and the deeper the level at which we invited them to share their experiences, the stronger the resistance became. It seemed to us that the resistance was stronger and better organized than the natural reticence of an individual to make disclosures to strangers, and we looked for some adequate explanation.

Our conclusion is that there exists in our culture a taboo, hitherto unrecognized as such, which prevents married couples from sharing their interpersonal experiences with other couples. We have called it the "intermarital taboo"; and when we describe it to groups of couples, they recognize at once what we are talking about.

Groups of married couples often form friendships with one another, enjoy social contacts, and work together on projects. However, there is always a tacit understanding that they don't reveal to one another, more than necessary, what is going on in their husband-wife relationships. To achieve this, complex mechanisms for evasion and mutual defense have been set up. Some of these are familiar—strong hostility (such as a kick on the shin under the table!) when the other seems to be revealing too much; making jokes to relieve tension when some inner secret of the marriage accidentally breaks to the surface; silence or withdrawal when "outsiders" appear to be probing too deeply. These defense systems work so well that it is not unusual, when the news breaks that a couple are involved in divorce proceedings, for other couples in their friendship circle to exclaim—"We are amazed! We had no idea that they were having trouble!"

We can easily think of good reasons for this taboo. It could be a protection against public humiliation because we all feel especially embarrassed about not being able to succeed in such a basic undertaking as marriage. It could be a safeguard against exploitation because a discontented marriage partner is often viewed as an easy conquest. It could be linked with our sexual taboos because any suggestion of sexual incompetence is deeply wounding to our pride. It could reflect the traditional view that the family is a closed in-group.

Our conclusion is that this taboo is being maintained with a strictness that is self-defeating to marriages in that it is depriving couples of help and support which they very much need from one another. So we deliberately encourage couples in our groups to relax their defenses and trust the group by sharing some of their interpersonal experiences with one another. When they do so, the effect is often dramatic. A sense of great warmth, empathy, mutual understanding, and support develops. We can often feel the tension in the group as they move up to the taboo, expressed as high-pitched, uneasy laughter. And then, when the group has moved into open sharing, this is replaced by a deep sense of comfortable relaxation.

Once the couples in the group have overcome this barrier, they rapidly identify with one another and eagerly share experiences. We often enjoy the enormous relief of a couple who discover that several others are also struggling with a difficulty which they had considered uniquely their own, and the loving solicitude with which a couple who have passed through some growth experience will try to help another couple who are still trying to find their way. As the couples share the directions in which they want their immediate future growth to carry them, they experience a very close sense of involvement with one another. It is a common experience for such a group of couples to say they feel closer to one another, after only a matter of hours spent together, than they do to other couples they have known for most of their married lives. Sometimes the group of couples, at the end of their experience together, will plan a reunion at some later date. And when they come together again, the sense of closeness and warmth immediately reasserts itself.

The bond which unites the couples in the group is not only forged by the experiences they have been through together. An additional element in it is their sense that they are bound together in a common purpose—to seek the enrichment of their own marriages. And as they end the group experience and return home, they do not suffer the loneliness which individual participants leaving an encounter group pass through. They go back as a social unit, to continue at home the process of enrichment which they have already begun. It is our distinct impression, though we have no statistical proof of it, that the casualty rates in marriage enrichment groups are low indeed compared with those in encounter groups.

There can be no question that the stimulus of group interaction between married couples furnishes a promising new means of promoting marriage enrichment on a widespread scale. Therapists are already using married couple groups as a highly effective means of treating seriously disturbed marriages. But the discovery of the equally high effectiveness of group interaction for couples with what would be classified as "good" and "stable" marriages, as a means of initiating them into new processes of growth together, seems to be something new.

The word is now getting around, and we confidently expect a great burgeoning of this movement. Already it is organized nationally, to our knowledge, by three religious bodies—The United Methodist Church uses the term Marriage Communication Labs;[2] the Catholic movement is called Marriage Encounter,[3] and has been described in a book[4] under that title by Antoinette Bosco; the Quaker project, which we initiated, speaks of Marriage Enrichment Retreats.[5] Other churches, together with the national YMCA, are increasingly interested. Apart from national organizations, a number of local organizations and agencies are running marriage enrichment programs, and their number is steadily increasing.

[2] The program is directed by Dr. Leon Smith. For information write Ministries in Marriage, The United Methodist Church, P.O. Box 871, Nashville, Tenn. 37202.

[3] Marriage Encounter, 5305 West Foster Avenue, Chicago, Ill. 60630.

[4] Antoinette Bosco, *Marriage Encounter: The Rediscovery of Love* (St. Meinrad, Ind.: Abbey Press, 1972).

[5] See the booklet *Marriage Enrichment Retreats: Story of a Quaker Project* by David and Vera Mace, published by Friends General Conference, 1520 Race Street, Philadelphia, Penn. 19102.

CHAPTER 17

Retreats for Marriage Enrichment

Both concepts and patterns of marriage enrichment vary widely among those who have developed this kind of project. The differences, however, are not basic. In fact, what impresses us again and again are the similarities. In this chapter and the next we shall describe our own experiences and conclusions.

It all began for us personally when Joe and Edith Platt, a Quaker couple who helped to run a retreat center called Kirkridge in the Pennsylvania Mountains near Bangor, invited us to conduct a weekend retreat for married couples. We were at that time joint executive directors of the American Association of Marriage Counselors, so this was a challenge we could hardly evade. Although we had been involved in many lectures and conferences about marriage and plenty of marriage counseling, a retreat for married couples was a new venture. With some trepidation, we accepted the invitation, conducted the retreat to the best of our ability, and learned a great deal in the process. This was in October, 1962.

The first Kirkridge retreat was successful enough to encourage the Platts to ask us to come again and again. We then began to receive other requests as it became known that we were available for this kind of leadership. The retreats began as a rule on Friday evening and ended with the noon meal on Sunday. We experimented with longer and shorter periods, including one lasting five full days. Our conclusion is that the weekend represents the best length of time for the average couple, and this has become our standard pattern. For pastors and their wives, we schedule the period from Monday evening to Wednesday noon. We have also met with groups of couples for separate evening sessions spaced out over four to six weeks. Limited seclusion and broken continuity make this decidedly less effective; but for couples who simply cannot get away from their homes, this is certainly better than nothing.

Kirkridge chose the term "retreat" in the first place, and we are aware that it has a religious connotation. We have however continued to use it because it represents very well what we have tried to offer—an opportunity for husband and wife to withdraw from their normal preoccupations and in an atmosphere of seclusion and relaxed leisure to take a long, searching look at themselves and their relationship to each other. If, however, the organization setting up the weekend prefers another title, we cheerfully call it a conference, workshop, or lab.

We have led couple groups under a wide variety of conditions—from quite luxurious accommodations to a somewhat primitive vacation home in the mountains where we slept under conditions of minimum privacy, washed in water from the creek, and retired to rough shelters in the woods to perform more private functions. Many retreats have been held in our home, the participants sleeping and eating at a nearby motel. Our experience strongly suggests that the most desirable setting is one that provides maximum seclusion. One weekend at a church, for example, proved exasperating because of the constant coming and going of other people. We also favor arrangements which protect the actual participants in the retreat from any but minimal organizing responsibilities.

We would regard five or six couples as the ideal size of group, but seldom have we enjoyed this luxury. Usually we have had to accept our upper limit of nine couples, apart from ourselves, making a total group of twenty. This has happened often because more couples applied than we could take, and it was hard not to accept the maximum number. Also, we find that family crises can compel couples to drop out unavoidably at the last moment, and two couples short in a retreat planned for five would leave only three. Our normal procedure has been to accept seven or eight couples.

Our request has been for couples who consider that they have reasonably good and stable marriages. We make it very clear that our purpose is not to provide therapy, but to encourage marital growth. We do not believe that group marital counseling should be attempted on a short-term basis; and although we would consider ourselves competent to undertake such counseling in the proper setting, it is no part of our purpose in these retreats. We also find that some couples come to the retreats with a good deal of apprehension, and they have sometimes told us that they would not have come at all without the assurance that this was not for problem couples. Despite all safeguards, however, couples with severe marital difficulties do occasionally get in under the wire, and we have to cope with this as best we can.

No requirements are set regarding age, race, vocation, education, or socioeconomic status. There are advantages in having a homogeneous group of couples; but there are also advantages in a heterogeneous group. Our retreats have included one engaged couple and one honeymooning couple who came straight from their wedding. They have also included retired couples. We have mingled highly qualified professionals with blue-collar workers, Ph.D.s with high school dropouts.

One firm condition is that husband and wife both attend—which means that if one has to drop out, both do so. And we insist that both continuously participate in the entire retreat, from beginning to end.

We are often asked about preparatory material for participants, especially books to read. We are willing to provide this if pressed, but we are hesitant about it. Recommending books might suggest that we are going to engage in intellectual discussion, which is not the case. The retreat is an adventure in sharing into which we all move together, ready to take it as it comes.

This will be a good point at which to discuss the leadership role. In this we have now had considerable experience—both in being leaders ourselves and in watching our trainees adjust to it. We would emphasize that leadership of these groups conforms to no stereotype and should not attempt to do so. It is a very individual matter, and each couple must find the way in which they can most comfortably "do their own thing."

Obviously married couples' groups can be led by an individual, and occasionally are. It is our view, however, that when the goal is marriage enrichment, there are great advantages in leadership being assumed by a married couple. The leaders thus themselves constitute a subgroup in a group of subgroups, so that identification is easy and natural in both directions. They also provide role models—not in the sense of presenting themselves as flawlessly perfect marriage partners (that might be rather disconcerting!), but rather as a couple who are themselves growing and desirous of growing further. The leaders themselves exemplify the quest for enrichment to which they are inviting the other couples; and if they make mistakes and admit it, this may be positively helpful. We have often been amused at the obvious enjoyment of the group when our teamwork temporarily faltered or broke down, and we revealed our feet of clay!

We do not attempt to take the role of experts or specialists, keeping ourselves at a different level from the other couples, as a therapist would normally do. Our concept of leadership is best expressed by the term "participating facilitators." Thus we do not hesitate to make ourselves vulnerable by sharing experiences in our own marriage which have been painful or humiliating; and if we find ourselves in conflict with each

134

other during the group session, we bring it out into the open and deal with it, just as we would expect any of the other couples to do.

It must be admitted, however, that leading this kind of retreat can be, for any couple, a challenging test of their capacity to work together. A breakdown in unity in the leaders could throw the entire group into disorder, much as the children in a family become confused when the parents demonstrate that they are in conflict with each other and unable to resolve it. Couples who lead these retreats should have a relationship to each other that is warm, secure, flexible, and positive.

The greatest hindrance to successful leadership, in our opinion, is anxiety and apprehension about how the retreat is going to turn out. We often suffered from this in our early experiences, and we are sure the groups concerned suffered too! In time we reached the point at which we saw clearly that unless we could have faith in the group's ability to find its own direction, our leadership could be a hindrance rather than a help. Clearly we must set the goal for the group, and we must hold them to it. But we could not predetermine how they would move toward that goal; nor could we set standards to define their level of performance. We could simply travel with them, confident that they would do their best.

Thus if we ever become concerned about what is happening, or not happening, or uncertain about what to do next, we do not withdraw for a private conference. We tell the group we are perplexed and ask them to help us. They always respond.

Once we had seen all this clearly, leadership of marriage enrichment groups became a pleasant and rewarding experience. We feel more relaxed in this role than in any other role involving responsibility. And we believe that this relaxation, which is a manifestation of our complete faith in the group, is what makes our leadership effective.

The time came when we felt we understood the process of group interaction between couples well enough to embark upon a program to train selected couples for leadership of marriage enrichment retreats. We were by this time receiving more invitations to lead retreats than we could possibly accept, and we decided to make the venture of training others who could extend what we had begun.

This was a Quaker program organized by Friends' General Conference. While some of the persons concerned were professionals, others were not. Our decision to train lay couples for leadership was not hastily made. After several years, however, we felt confident that we could go ahead. Although we expected criticism from some of our professional colleagues, this has not in fact developed to any significant degree, and we are now entirely satisfied that we were justified in taking a calculated risk. After all, our trainees were not attempting therapy as normally defined, so they were not invading professional territory. We know of no case where our lay couples have encountered crisis situations which they were unable to handle with wisdom and skill.

The training of the Quaker couples was relatively simple. They were carefully selected by their Yearly Meetings from all over the United States and Canada and brought to Pendle Hill near Philadelphia, where we all participated in a retreat. The actual retreat sessions were supplemented by instruction and discussions concerning the leadership role. The couples then returned home, and their Yearly Meetings set up retreats for them in their own regions. Six months after the first training retreat, they all came back to Pendle Hill for a report and follow-up weekend, at which any difficulties they had encountered were fully discussed. Two successive groups received this preparation. During the second round, two years after the first, we were aided by two highly experienced and capable couples from the first round, who then took over the further supervision of the trainees. All reports on the continued leadership of these trainee couples have been satisfactory.

The wide geographical separation of these particular couples forced us to settle for a minimal program. We have since worked out a more adequate plan for couples within reasonable distance of each other. We would favor a couple under consideration for training participating first in two or three retreats conducted by skilled leaders. Then, if the leaders all judged them to have good potential, they should function as coleaders of two or three further retreats, again with experienced couples. The third step would be for them to share leadership with one or two other trainee couples with a similar degree of experience to their own. Finally, if all went well, they could be permitted to lead retreats by themselves.

Along these lines, we believe it would be possible, in orderly fashion, to select and train all the leaders necessary to sustain the growing demand for marriage enrichment groups which we confidently expect in the next few years. However, to organize this effectively we decided that it was necessary to set up the national organization which we shall describe later in this book.

CHAPTER 18

What Happens in the Group?

We are now ready to describe a typical retreat—except that there is no such thing as a typical retreat! All we can describe is what we typically do. That will furnish a mere skeleton. It is the particular people who take part who make the experience what it is, and their uniqueness decides the uniqueness of what happens.

There isn't even a typical procedure because we are always experimenting with new ideas—sometimes ideas suggested by the couples taking part. Just as our trainees depart from what they see us do and invent new ways of their own, so we also depart from what we used to do and invent new ways of our own. No description therefore is adequate. Only the experience can tell you what a marriage enrichment retreat is like.

If possible we all take the evening meal on Friday together. After we have eaten, we sit round in a circle, husbands and wives side by side. They have been told in advance to wear informal clothes.

As leaders, we offer a few words of explanation. We ask if anyone is feeling apprehensive and would be helped by asking questions. Then we explain that we like to spend the whole of the first evening getting to know each other as couples. By doing this we shall get over any feelings of strangeness and feel comfortable and relaxed together.

Some leaders do this by giving each couple paper and

crayons, have them draw together a picture of their marriage, and then take turns in explaining the picture to the others. We prefer what we call the questioning method.

The conventional "getting acquainted" procedure when people assemble for meetings is to go around the circle and allow each to give his name and basic information about himself. A more stiff and stilted procedure it would be hard to imagine! We never "go round the circle" for *any* purpose; nor do we ever "call on people" in alphabetical order. In fact, we never call on people at all. We ask for volunteers, and they set their own order. It would be theoretically possible for a couple to sit right through one of our retreats without saying a word. In fact, it once happened! A very bashful Pennsylvania Dutch couple asked if they could participate without joining in the discussions. This was agreed, and they did. At the end they shook hands all around very cordially and said they had had a wonderful experience and would have plenty to say at their next retreat!

Nor do we ask people to tell us about themselves. It is much more important that *we* ask what *we* want to know about the others. So we take turns, as couples, at being questioned about ourselves by the whole group. And it is understood that we can go on questioning each other during the entire weekend, in or out of formal sessions. Very personal questions can be asked, but all questions need not be answered.

As the leading couple, we always offer ourselves for questioning first. In doing so, we explain that we, and all the others, are to be called by our first names at all times. Anyone being addressed in a more formal manner may exact a fine of a dollar on the spot.

The questioning begins, and when they are satisfied, we invite another couple to take our places. So we continue till all have had their turn. This invariably takes the whole evening —indeed, we often have to set time limits to avoid going on too late. We urge the couples to get to bed early and fall asleep going over the names and identities of the others in the group.

On Saturday morning we assemble for a three-hour session with a break at some convenient point. We explain our practice of beginning every session by asking for "concerns"—an expressive Quaker term which means that if you have anything on your mind, you may and should express it. This includes any negative feeling about something that has happened in the group, any personal uneasiness, any feeling that we ought to be doing something differently. The importance of getting these feelings out in the open is that otherwise the fellowship of the group is broken. We think it is important that married couples should always take time to hear each other's concerns; so how can we better make our point than by building this into the group process? A concern always gets priority, and we stay with it until we clear it up. It is even possible to have a concern that someone else in the group has a concern and isn't expressing it!

We now remind the group of our purpose—to look honestly at our marriages and consider how we can enrich them—and ask where they want to begin. At this point the group may flounder a little because they expected to be told what to do. However, they soon come up with ideas, and we put these down on an agenda and decide which item they want to take first. A few false starts don't matter at this point; they may even help the group to take responsibility for itself. It is the responsibility of the leaders, however, to sense as quickly as possible what the needs of the group are, how able and willing they are to get into real sharing about their marriages, and to help them to get going. If there are couples present who have had previous experience of retreats, they can be of great help in moving the group along at this point.

A very insecure group will begin at the level of intellectual discussion and choose some "safe" subject—working wives, troublesome teen-agers, money management, and the like. It may be necessary for the group to start at this level, testing one another out to see how directly personal they can venture to be. If the group can't move to the personal issues, the leaders must play their facilitating role with some such questions as, "I wonder why we're discussing this question. Mary, you started it. Was that because this is something you and John have been working on?" If this proves to be the case, Mary and John may feel able to explain how the issue is affecting them. Then one of the leaders may ask, "Did any other couple identify with Mary's and John's situation?" This may lead to further sharing at the personal level.

This is not manipulating the group. We have told them plainly that our purpose is to share experiences, not opinions. We have acknowledged that it may be difficult to get started with this because it may involve some of us in making ourselves vulnerable, and we can do this only when we trust one another. We ask all the couples to be willing, as far as they are able, to make ventures in this direction. But we also assure them that no pressure will be put on them. They must *volunteer* to contribute their experiences and need only tell as much as they comfortably can.

We have developed a number of exercises that can help. For example, we might ask Mary and John, instead of telling the group about their difficulty, to turn to each other and dialogue it together while the rest of us listen. This goes a long way toward personalizing the issue, and other couples who have identified with Mary and John may be invited to dialogue together as well. If the group is timid about getting into this, we ourselves will dialogue to show them what we mean.

Dialogue can be used specifically to get the discussion going at the right level. Typical topics that have been put on our agendas are: "How to deal with conflict in marriage"; "What about decision-making?" "How do we meet each other's dependency needs?" "What can you do about jealousy in a marriage partner?" These could all be discussed in general terms. But they can also be discussed through dialogue. A good way is to ask three couples to volunteer to do this. They can remain sitting where they are, but a better way is to have them sit on the floor or on chairs in the middle of the circle, each couple in turn talking over the question as it affects them while the others sit in silence (interruptions or laughter can be distracting). Then, when the three couples have finished, the others can join in.

Many other exercises have been devised, and leaders are constantly inventing new ones. A special favorite of ours, which we often use to close the Saturday evening session, is what we call positive interaction. We usually explain the procedure in advance and ask three couples to volunteer. They sit in the center facing each other and holding hands. Then in turn they simply tell each other some of the things they especially like about each other. It is as simple as that. Yet it is highly effective and can be very moving and heartwarming. Surprisingly enough, studies of marital interaction have shown that couples spend much more time telling each other what they *don't* like about each other than what they *do* like, despite the fact that we have strong evidence that praise achieves much more than blame in improving interpersonal relationships. So we like to include this exercise in most of our retreats, and we invite all the other couples to do it in the privacy of their own rooms.

We must however get back to the timetable. We always give the participants time off on Saturday afternoon, reassembling about three-thirty. The couples may do what they like—rest, walk, drive—but they also have an assignment to fulfill. We borrowed this procedure from the Catholic Marriage Encounter and have adapted it. Toward the end of the morning, we take fifteen minutes to ask each of the participants to write down, privately and quite spontaneously, five things he likes about his marriage, five things he would like to see improved, and five things he could himself do to improve the relationship. They then keep these individual lists until they are alone together in the afternoon, when they are asked to share and discuss them to whatever extent, and in whatever way, they wish. When the group reassemble later in the afternoon, we invite any who are willing to do so to report to us on their encounter. The session then continues until the evening meal and resumes afterwards. We try to close in reasonable time, so that couples can if necessary continue their private encounter and try some positive interaction before retiring.

Another three-hour session on Sunday morning concludes the retreat. In the final hour the couples are asked, after ten minutes of consultation together, to report on what new insights they have gained, what they see as the directions in which they will seek the future enrichment of their marriages, and what help they might need in doing so. The group will now have spent from twelve to fifteen hours together in sessions, as well as their social interaction between sessions and their private couple encounters. In our opinion this period of time is just about right for a good deal to be achieved before fatigue sets in. Although the experience is intensive, it is not normally intense, and couples often tell us at the end that they feel relaxed and refreshed. The amount of warmth and mutual love that develops in some groups has to be experienced to be believed.

Since we have referred to the importance of personalizing the group discussion, it may be appropriate to conclude this chapter with a few brief summaries to illustrate what this experience has done for some couples:

> • A young pastor and his wife, who participated in one of our early retreats, not only found their marriage renewed, but decided together that they should devote themselves henceforth to the cause of marriage enrichment as the most worthwhile use they could make of their lives. The pastor

pulled up stakes, underwent professional training in marriage counseling, took a doctoral degree in the field, and now directs a center for marriage preparation and counseling.

• A newlywed couple (already mentioned above) came to one of our retreats for the first part of their honeymoon. Several years later they enrolled for another retreat we were conducting. They spoke with gratitude and enthusiasm of their honeymoon experience, saying it had launched them in a marriage that had been deeply rewarding to them both. Their contribution to this second retreat was outstanding and deeply influenced several other participating couples.

• A pastor and his wife came to a retreat and revealed that they were involved in a serious conflict. He wanted to resign from his church, she was bitterly opposed to this, and they were in a state of complete deadlock. Other couples in the group shared their experiences of decision-making, the issues were clarified, and the couple went home happy and reconciled.

• Two young people had broken their engagement as a result of a conflict they couldn't resolve, but came to a retreat in the hope that more experienced couples could help them. They presented the whole issue to the entire group on the Saturday night, and at the Sunday morning session, relaxed and radiant, reported that the conflict had been resolved.

• A Quaker couple, who had already been working with married couples in their home community, came to a marriage enrichment retreat and were so convinced of its value that they took the following summer off and traveled extensively across the continent, from one Quaker Meeting to another, holding meetings in which they shared their new insights.

• A couple who already had a good marriage realized, as a result of the retreat they attended, that they ought to do more to share their experience with others. Besides making themselves available for marriage enrichment programs, the wife wrote a book on marriage which has since been published.

• In a dialogue on decision-making at one of our retreats, a couple brought out their acute conflict about whether to have a child. The husband had children by a previous marriage, was opposed to having more, and had apparently failed to understand the intensity of his wife's frustration. In the course of a dialogue in which another couple joined in very helpfully, a tangle of misunderstandings was cleared up and the dialogue ended with the problem solved and the couple rapturously embracing each other.

• A couple who had considered their marriage a good one became aware, at the retreat they attended, that their levels of communication were really quite superficial. Following the retreat, they developed a much deeper and richer relationship, setting aside a period every day for open sharing of all thoughts and feelings. Five years later, they are increasingly involved in leading marriage enrichment programs in their state.

From these and other illustrations, it would appear that marriage enrichment programs commonly have four results:

1. *A new awareness of growth potential in marriage.* This is what happens to most couples who participate. Their static concept of marriage is replaced by a dynamic concept. They see their relationship in a new and different light. Possibilities of greater depth and closeness open up for them, and they are shown how to realize these possibilities. Not all of them follow through, but our later contacts with couples who have participated in retreats suggest that a high proportion of them do.

2. *The discovery that few couples have unique difficulties.* Because of the intermarital taboo, couples often form the impression that some of their personal problems of communication and adjustment are such as no other couple could possibly

145

be experiencing. This creates in them feelings of guilt, of embarrassment, of isolation. When one couple hesitatingly venture to share such a difficulty in the group, only to discover that several other couples immediately respond and identify with them, the sense of relief engendered all round is very reassuring. Most of us greatly fear the remotest possibility that we may be abnormal; and the little troubles we experience in our marriage relationships become far less terrifying when we find that other couples are in the same situation after all.

3. *The clearing away of some obstacles to growth.* Although we confine our retreats to couples with basically good marriages, it often turns out that these marriages are in fact not growing and that the cause lies in some unresolved area of conflict. In the atmosphere of open sharing, they become acutely aware of the barrier that prevents them from achieving relationship-in-depth; and the encouragement and support of the other couples provide them with strong motivation to make a real effort to clear it up. Not all these conflicts emerge openly. Sometimes a couple will approach one of the leaders privately and ask for help. Occasionally they will report to the group that in a late night sitting they have cleared up a long-standing problem in their relationship, without specifying what the problem was. There have been couples who left retreats deeply dissatisfied with their relationship, and afterwards sought marriage counseling which they had needed before but had avoided. Large numbers of married couples in our culture know that their marriages, though apparently stable, are superficial and disappointing; but they lack the motivation to act resolutely in moving the relationship to deeper levels—often instead turning to substitute satisfactions outside the marriage to ease their frustrations. Marriage enrichment experiences often seem to provide the needed motivation to couples who have already taken the first step by participating in a retreat.

4. *A sense of vocation to help others.* One of the sterling qualities in human nature is our desire, when we have dis-

covered something good that we had hitherto lacked, to pass on the good news to others so that they also may enjoy the same benefits. We have quoted several instances of couples whose response to a marriage enrichment retreat was to do just this. One effect of the taboo on the sharing of marital experiences with other couples is an unnecessary and exaggerated privatism about marriage, with the result that many young people today state in all sincerity that they don't believe in marriage because they have never seen a really happy couple. Incredible as it may seem, this can be literally true. It has been said that broken marriages are news, but happy marriages are of no interest to anyone. Many of the couples who have attended our retreats think otherwise, and they have sought and found ways to work for the propagation of the concept of marriage as relationship-in-depth. We have been greatly encouraged by this and believe it may be opening up new and hitherto unrealized possibilities of mutual support and help which married couples can offer one another.

We conclude this chapter with a brief discussion of a question we are often asked: namely, how do our marriage enrichment retreats differ from encounter groups? The obvious difference is that encounter groups are composed of individuals while our groups are confined to and led by married couples. This means a greater complexity in the leadership and a greater complexity in the group itself. The encounter group is confined to interactions between separate individuals, usually individuals who have not met before and will not have any continuing association afterwards. By contrast, we have multidimensional interactions—between individuals in the group, between couples (including the leading couple) within the group, and between husband and wife within each marital unit.

There is another difference which concerns procedures. In some encounter groups at least, confrontation tactics are used which aim at arousing anger or fear with the idea of bringing

147

these emotions to the surface so that they may be expressed
and examined. We recognize that many people in our culture
suffer as a result of undue suppression of emotions and that
properly controlled opportunities to bring these feelings to the
surface may be therapeutic.

We take the view, however, that it would not be appropriate
to encourage this kind of activity in our retreats. A weekend
may provide too short a time adequately to resolve the consequences of such cathartic release. Anyway, we consider this
to be a task that belongs properly in the field of therapy, and
our leading couples are not necessarily qualified to undertake
this. Besides, anything of this kind would run the risk of di-
verting the retreat from its major goal.

This does not mean, of course, that feelings of hostility do
not arise between marriage partners in the group. They do,
and we accept them. Indeed, one of our frequent tasks is to
encourage the couples to share with each other how they deal
with hostile feelings that arise naturally in their marriages.
What we do not do is to use devices to foment hostile feeling.

Our emphasis, as already indicated, is always on growth,
and in this context we find it best to stress positive rather than
negative emotions. In doing this we have found that when
positive interaction is encouraged, negative feelings, even
when they are deep and intense, tend to dissolve and wither
away. Couples have told us how their fierce hate melted in
the atmosphere of warm and loving support that developed
in the group. The result was that, with the stirring of com-
passion within them, they began to see each other in a new
light.

The problem of getting rid of inappropriate anger is indeed a critical one for us all, and especially in marriage. We
take issue, however, with the often stressed notion that anger
can only be overcome by being discharged. We suggest that
we may have been neglecting the therapeutic power of love
not only to cast out fear, but to dissolve hostility.

CHAPTER 19

Couples Helping One Another

When we ask ourselves what it is that happens in a marriage enrichment retreat, the answer is very clear. It isn't that the leaders impart earthshaking new knowledge to the couples, though they may offer a little homespun wisdom here and there. It isn't that they put formidable clinical skills to work as a group therapist does. All that the leaders do is to act as facilitators, releasing for the mutual benefit of the couples *resources that are already there.*

Something similar happened in England many years ago in the preparation of engaged couples for marriage. After organizing lectures for the couples and planning individual counseling interviews for them, it was discovered that much more could be achieved by putting the couples in small groups led by marriage counselors and letting them help one another. They did this to very good purpose. In one group a couple were told firmly but kindly by all the others that they just didn't have what it takes to achieve a successful marriage and they had better face it and break up—which they did!

The power of couples to help one another has also been demonstrated over and over again in therapy groups. If a marriage is really sick, it can get this kind of help.

What has never been done before, on any significant scale, is for ordinary married couples to band together to help one another in the vital business of developing good, healthy, happy marriages. Why not?

There are three reasons why this hasn't been done.

First, because we have stubbornly refused to face the fact that achieving good, healthy, happy marriages, in terms of the deep intimacy and rich companionship we look for in marriage today, is really difficult. It is in fact so difficult that the great majority of people are failing in it. It is simply absurd and terribly costly to go on arrogantly refusing to face the fact that we *all* need help if we are to achieve in marriage what we need and want.

What we found in the couples who came to our retreats was that many of these couples, who had what they and others considered good and stable marriages, were in fact settling for relationships that were far short of their inherent potential. Some exhibited the same self-defeating interaction patterns which we were accustomed to finding in couples with problems—but either they had resigned themselves to accepting these poor patterns as the best they could hope for, or the conflicts that resulted had not yet reached crisis proportions.

Matching our observation of these couples with some of the research findings on marital interaction, we arrived at four conclusions:

1. Only a small proportion of marriages come anywhere near to being really good. Lederer and Jackson[1] suggest that the proportion of "stable-satisfactory" marriages in the United States today does not exceed 5 to 10 percent. Other studies have come up with similar estimates.

2. Most married couples desire and hope for the achievement of what we have called relationship-in-depth. Early in their married life, however, they find their growth together blocked by interpersonal conflicts which they either cannot

---

[1] Lederer and Jackson, *The Mirages of Marriage,* p. 129.

understand or are unable to resolve. They settle for a series of compromises resulting in a superficial relationship.

3. As time passes, the couple either accept this unsatisfactory situation or it becomes progressively intolerable. They are usually so locked into their self-defeating interaction pattern that they are quite unable to change it by their own unaided efforts. Some seek marriage counseling, but often too late for it to be effective.

4. The tragedy of undeveloped potential could be avoided in many instances if married couples had a clearer concept of the task of marriage and did not have to struggle in almost total isolation from other couples going through the same experience.

The second reason why couples have not joined together to help one another in their marital growth is referred to in the last of these conclusions. The intermarital taboo blocks real, honest communication between them. The taboo makes the inner life of each individual marriage so private and personal that the married couple are compelled to go it alone—at least until their situation is so desperate that it drives them to seek help of some kind, by which time it is often too late to do much about it.

Experience has proved that people who climb dangerous mountains can avoid many grave hazards by being linked together by a long rope. Imagine a situation in which someone convinced the climbers that it was a sign of weakness and cowardice to be roped to others, and it became customary for them to climb alone, with the result that many of them slipped over precipices and tumbled into crevasses. That would exactly parallel the way we are now behaving about marriage.

We are not advocating abandonment of the proper and protective privacy that belongs to the marriage relationship. We do not favor doing away altogether with the taboo. But it needs to be eased considerably, for in its present strict and extreme form it is doing much more harm than good. And our retreats furnish convincing proof that when, under properly controlled conditions, a group of married couples can let down some of their defenses, the result, far from being disastrous, is highly beneficial.

The third reason for the failure of couples to help one another is that they have never organized themselves for this purpose. Indeed, apart from purely social activities, married people seem never to have organized themselves for any serious purpose whatsoever. Yet it is almost impossible to think of any other groups of people in our society who have common interests and who have *not* banded themselves together for the promotion or defense of those interests. The only possible explanation we can offer, since the major common interest of married people is to succeed in marriage, is that a strong psychological force has up to now prevented their coming together—and this force is of course the intermarital taboo.

So the provision of services for married couples has hitherto been undertaken without either their support or cooperation. This is true of services for marriage preparation and for marriage counseling. We have even heard complaints from wives of marriage counselors that their husbands were so busy counseling couples in trouble that their own marriages were being neglected. And frequently we have encountered marriage counselors, working together in the same community, who had never even met one another's husbands or wives!

The marriage enrichment concept must challenge all this. Marriages in our culture are failing at an increasing rate, in spite of the formidable array of professional practitioners who are busily engaged in remedial work. Surely it is time the married couples, especially those who are enjoying creative and deeply satisfying relationships, got into the act.

Since marriage enrichment retreats have proved their worth, there is no reason why they should not now be organized on a massive scale. Certainly many couples are fearful of becoming involved, but the warm advocacy of other couples who have been through the experience could soon allay their fears. As one of our lay group leaders put it, "The underlying problem is the fact that the marriage enrichment retreat meets *unfelt* needs. To get the tingle of a potential deepening and enriching takes emotional impact. This means hearing from someone obviously sensible who is warmly convinced about it." [2] The Catholics have done this very effectively by organizing parish meetings at which couples who have been involved in Marriage Encounter tell other couples what it has meant to them.[3]

We are now convinced that genuine interest in marriage enrichment can quite easily be aroused. The idea, logically presented, makes sense. For some time now in our own locality we have had a waiting list of couples desiring to attend retreats.

There is no major problem involved in setting up these retreats. They can be held almost anywhere—in a motel, a camp, even a home. Their organization is very simple. All the office work needed is a brief statement, giving basic information, mailed out to the couples in advance. No extra strain is placed on professional manpower, since lay couples can be trained for leadership if necessary.

What is needed is to bring together a dedicated group of convinced married couples who will take responsibility for getting on with the job. This, as we see it, will be the primary task of the Association of Couples for Marriage Enrichment.

The power of couples to help one another need not be confined to arranging retreats. Once in action, they can take on other greatly needed tasks. They can organize programs of marriage preparation for young couples considering marriage,

---

[2] Quoted in *Marriage Enrichment Retreats: Story of a Quaker Project,* p. 22. See chapter 16, note 5.
[3] See Bosco, *Marriage Encounter: The Rediscovery of Love.*

who would probably respond to an invitation from a group of married couples more readily than to one from a professional agency. They can set up "first aid" services for couples in serious trouble—we have evidence that when a mature married couple sit down with another couple in bad trouble, a great deal of healing can take place. This does not mean of course that the couple would undertake counseling as such, but they could work as aides to get couples in need to competent professional counselors and in follow-up work after counseling. A local group of couples could also investigate marriage counseling resources in their community and make this information available to those who need it.

In summary, what we are saying is that the cause of promoting good marriages can now be taken up and carried forward by the people obviously best motivated and equipped for the task—*the couples who themselves have growing marriages*. It is really surprising that this has never been done before. It can be done now; and we believe we are about to witness what someone has aptly called "the irresistible power of an idea whose time has come."

CHAPTER 20

Married Couples, Unite!

In this book we are trying to say something to our readers—
something which we consider to be of very great importance.

We sense a mood of pessimism about marriage. It seems to
be based on a mistaken idea—that marriage is a weary, totter-
ing, declining institution, an anachronism destined soon to
become obsolete and to be replaced with something else.

We reject this idea because we consider it to be a serious
misinterpretation of the facts. The rigid institutional, hierarchical marriage of the past is dying, yes. But in its place
is emerging, phoenix-like, a new and quite different form
which we call the companionship marriage—a mutually creative, flexible, in-depth sharing of life, a partnership of equals.
This new marriage offers what most couples, according to our
observation and experience, long to achieve for themselves.

But it is difficult to achieve. Much more difficult than the
traditional form. So difficult that tens of thousands are failing
in the attempt, becoming disillusioned, and giving up.

This need not happen. Many of these couples *could* succeed. But not without new understanding. Not without training in unaccustomed patterns of communicating with each
other, interacting with each other; not without removing the
barriers to a life of deep intimacy, trust, and love; not without
serious, intelligent, and sustained effort. The goal is attain-
able, but the price is high.

Nevertheless, plenty of couples seem ready and eager to make the venture. We are convinced of this. We have found it to be so in our marriage enrichment retreats. This knowledge has encouraged us to examine what is happening to marriage, on the outside and on the inside. We have reported some of our findings in this book.

We have considered, also, whether it would be possible to launch a program to get this encouraging news to millions of couples who are faltering and giving up. We see no practical reason why this should not be done. Not all will respond, of course. But we believe many will. And we believe they should be given the chance to do so.

What *is* this program? It is essentially a shift in our whole emphasis, a change of direction from negative to positive in what we are offering to married couples—from static to dynamic, from remedial to preventive, from inertia to active pursuit of growth.

How can this be done? It will require new resources. But we already have them. We are simply not using them, or not using them efficiently. We are squandering money, manpower, and time on programs that bring poor returns. We have no sensible policy, no sound strategy. We are simply drifting, clutching at straws, taking ineffectual steps in unproductive directions. What we need to do is to formulate a comprehensive program to offer all necessary help to all couples who want better marriages and are prepared to work for them. It must be a sound program. It must be convincing. It must work. We believe it can be done.

Who will get this going? That is the problem. It should all have been done long ago. It wasn't done because not enough people saw the issue clearly and not enough people cared enough.

We think that can be changed. We think there *are* people who care enough. But they can't act until they are organized. We propose to organize them.

156

Who *are* these people? They are married couples. Couples who believe in marriage, because for them personally marriage is not a trap, not a state of misery, not an obsolete institution. Marriage for them is good. It is rewarding. It is fulfilling. They believe in it. They are ready to say so. They would welcome the chance to stand up and be counted.

Nobody has ever asked this of married couples before— to join together and affirm their faith in marriage. Some of them have been indignant as they have listened to the abuse and scorn, the cynicism and skepticism, that have been poured out in attacks on marriage. They have wished they had some way of answering back, of rebuttal. But they have felt helpless —unable to speak because they had no voice, unable to act because they had no power.

We plan to offer them a voice, to offer them power. Other groups in our society have found a way to be heard, a way to act. The way is—to organize. Youth have organized and have been heard. Women have organized and have been heard. Labor has organized and has been heard. Blacks have organized and have been heard. Retired persons have organized and have been heard.

Why have married couples never organized? Because marriage, as we have pointed out, has been nobody's business. Because it is private. Because it is personal. Because it is taboo. Therefore no one has represented it. No one has defended it. It has been ridiculed, laughed at, kicked around, mocked. And there has been no response. Or rather, there have been a million individual and separate responses, but they have not been heard. Because there was no way of making a united response.

This may sound as if we are summoning married couples to man the barricades, to picket the U.S. Congress, to march on Washington. That is not the idea—although it *could* be part of the idea if it ever came to be necessary. We are not inviting married couples to unite in order to battle the opposition, to assert our rights, to demand new laws or special privileges or more money. We will unite not in order to *get,* but in order to *give.* We will unite not to argue something, but to demonstrate something. Our purpose will not be to blame the state or the professionals for having done a poor job, but to offer to help them do a better job. Our primary object will not be to talk, but to work. To work together for better marriages, beginning with our own.

So we have decided to start a new national organization. We hope it will eventually become international. We are taking this step after long thought and with deep conviction. Our decision is not a new idea. In fact, we first thought of it over a quarter of a century ago. On the liner *Queen Elizabeth,* crossing the Atlantic in December, 1947, one of us wrote these words:

> We have been so furtive and secretive about our married happiness that many people have grown cynical about marriage altogether. It has been said and written that marriage is an overrated and outmoded institution; and the tens of thousands of gloriously happy married people have never raised their voices to deny it. I have been told in all seriousness by an able man and a keen observer of human affairs that he had scarcely ever in his life come in contact with a successful marriage. Why, I said to myself, are the best married people hiding their light under a bushel? Is it not time that some of them emerged from the seclusion of their happy, peaceful homes, and began to "sell" marriage to a generation rapidly becoming cynical and disillusioned about it? [1]

Why did we not act on this idea before? Why wait a quarter of a century? We think the climate would not have been favorable at that time. And we had no central concept on which to focus then. We have now. The concept is marriage enrich-

---

[1] Mace, *Marriage Counseling,* p. 149.

ment. We find that it is a concept which brings a warm and positive response.

So we believe the time has come. We must act now. We shall have acted by the time these words appear in print. We shall have started ACME, the Association of Couples for Marriage Enrichment. If you are a couple who believe in the concept of marriage enrichment, if reading this book has convinced you that this is something you believe in, we invite you to join us. In the next chapter we will tell you what ACME is all about.

CHAPTER 21

A National Association for Marriage Enrichment

The concept of the Association of Couples for Marriage Enrichment has been worked out in numerous discussions with a great variety of married couples and with many wise and experienced professional people. Reactions have varied. Some were cautious, others were enthusiastic. Some found it such a startlingly new idea that they needed time to think about it before they were ready to offer an opinion. There were various views about how successful it might prove to be. What is interesting, and hopeful, is that no one has been entirely negative about it. Those not wholly convinced have been inclined to say, "Why not try it and see what happens?"

The name has raised considerable controversy. We have been reminded that grocery stores, laundries, barbershops, snack bars, and a variety of other establishments are called ACME. But in the end we decided that it was too good a name to be surrendered to commercial interests, and we were not likely to be confused with any of them. We know of no other *organization* with these initials, although we will no doubt be informed in due course that there are dozens of them. We are aware that the letters are the same as those in our name, and that this might be interpreted as vanity on our part. We dismiss this as unimportant, a purely accidental coincidence.

We wanted to keep ACME because it expresses a noble ideal. It is a Greek word meaning the highest point, the summit, the peak. The American Heritage Dictionary defines it as "the point of utmost attainment." The verb *acmazo,* which occurs once in the New Testament, refers to growing things achieving their fullest maturity. In Russian literature, a group called the Acmeists set themselves the goal of bringing poetry to high levels of perfection. So the word expresses very appropriately the concept of married couples reaching upward together toward the achievement of their highest potential.

Membership in ACME is open to any couple, either married or preparing for marriage, without distinction of race, creed, class, vocation, or age, who are prepared to make a commitment to the following four objectives:

1. To seek together to become equal partners in a loving, sharing, and mutually creative relationship.

2. To join with other ACME members in activities and experiences designed to promote mutual growth and enrichment.

3. To help to provide and to promote in our community effective services to foster better marriages.

4. To work to improve the public image of marriage as a relationship capable of promoting both personal growth and mutual fulfillment.

These four objectives emerged out of many discussions. They represent the kind of commitment that can be made by the kind of couple likely to want to join us. All ACME member couples will renew their commitment yearly on their wedding anniversary.

Member couples will pay dues at the rate of a dollar a month, or $12 annually. We consider this to be a figure any concerned couple would be able to afford. All income will of course be used to further the growth of ACME and the projects it decides to undertake. A newsletter will go out regularly to all members, and when we can afford it this will grow into a magazine or journal, with news items, articles, and reviews of books and other materials. In time, we hope ACME will produce other publications.

We have created an auxiliary membership category— ACME Associates—for individuals who believe in our purposes and wish to support us, but are not in a position to join on a couple basis. This includes unmarried professionals whose work involves them in dealing with married couples; widowed and divorced persons; and husbands or wives whose spouses, for one reason or another, are not yet ready to join with them on a couple basis. ACME associates pay the same $12.00 annual dues as couple members, receive all mailings, and may participate in activities which are not specifically couple-based. They may not however vote or hold office.

ACME will be allowed to grow at its own pace. But of course the first order of business will be the recruitment of new members, and we shall actively try to make contact with couples likely to be interested. With increasing numbers will come increasing strength, and as our income grows we should be able to build a strong and effective organization with an appropriate national headquarters and staff. One optimist pointed out that if we enrolled 100,000 couples, we would have a working budget of over a million dollars! That seems a long way off at present, though it could happen. (Parents Without Partners already is reported to have a national membership of 95,000.) However, our concept of ACME is that it will function fully, for the benefit of those who belong to it, at any and every stage of its development.

We see the real strength of ACME in terms of local chapters all over the country. Any group of member couples in a community can form a chapter. In time local chapters will combine into state and regional divisions of ACME, with elected officers at each level. In the meantime, we have already appointed national officers and couples who will serve as state representatives in both the United States and Canada.

The local chapters will be free to develop their own programs, on an experimental basis, until experience shows us the most effective ways of working. The first task is likely to be the organizing of retreats and growth groups for ACME members and other married couples. At first, this may mean bringing in experienced couples from outside to lead retreats until suitable local couples have been trained. A plan for such training, and for appropriate certification, is being worked out. We shall have to be careful, in our beginning phase, to temper our eagerness to move ahead with the need to maintain high standards of competence.

In due course, local chapters will be able to assess their community resources in terms of services to married couples and to couples preparing for marriage. ACME will be a citizens' organization, and one of its obvious tasks will be to check out available professional services for quality and effectiveness. Where these are good, ACME will support them. Where they are questionable, ACME will have a right to investigate. In some communities, unfortunately, there are incompetent and fraudulent marriage counselors, and ACME, after due consideration, may be compelled to bring the facts to light. Responsible professional organizations are doing their best to expose malpractice, and ACME could give them valuable assistance.

Obviously ACME chapters will want to work closely with professionals—marriage counselors, family life educators, physicians, clergymen, social workers, and others—who are in any way involved in the promotion of better marriages. Professionals and their spouses are of course welcome to join ACME, under exactly the same conditions as other couples. ACME will, however, have no hierarchies of membership, no special categories. All will be on the same level, participating together in the pursuit of the primary goals.

The ACME commitment includes the possibility that the association may act as a lobby or pressure group. We think the possibility of such action should be approached very cautiously. To take positions on controversial issues could easily divide our ranks and divert ACME from its primary task. However, we could act vigorously on a clear-cut issue of common concern, such as gross misrepresentation and villification of marriage in the mass media, or some public policy which manifestly discriminated against married couples.

We see the long-term task of ACME as being to join with the state and with the professionals in providing a "third force" in the vitally important task of steering marriage through a period of crisis and change, of providing all possible help to couples struggling to make their marriages work, and above all of setting up an effective program of prevention, guidance, and training for couples from the beginning of their association throughout their entire life together. We believe that those who are already striving to achieve these goals could be powerfully fortified if a large and united group of married couples, themselves dedicated to seek growth in their own relationship, can get into the act. We think it is not too much to claim that such action could take us a considerable distance in the direction of establishing better families and a better society.

Our own role in ACME is that of its founders. In launching it we have fulfilled a hope first conceived a quarter of a century ago. We cannot predict how effective our ideas will prove to be, but we are ready to see them put to the test. Whether or not ACME will succeed will depend largely on the number of couples who see in it a movement in which they want to be involved, a cause they can believe in and support. If many see it in this light, it could become a large organization and have a wide influence. But even if only a few do so, it will serve a vital purpose in supporting and promoting the marriage enrichment movement. Our personal intention is that as soon as ACME is securely established, we shall hand it over to the leaders who will naturally have emerged by that time. We do not wish to encourage the cult of personalities. We have spent most of our lives working together for better marriages, and launching ACME seems a fitting way to bring these activities to a close before we rest from our labors.

[*Postcript on Joining ACME.* Information and membership forms may be obtained by writing to ACME, 403 S. Hawthorne Road, Winston-Salem, N.C. 27103. This is the address of the Behavioral Sciences Center of the Bowman Gray School of Medicine, where we serve professionally on the staff of the Marital Health Clinic. We acknowledge with gratitude the cooperation of Dr. Clark E. Vincent, Director of the Center and of the Clinic, in allowing the national office to be housed there. He and his wife were among the first to join ACME, and they are deeply committed to its purposes and goals.]

Epilogue

You have been reading a book about making marriages better. Could *anything* add more to the sum of human happiness?

Surely, you say, there are more important achievements. A cure for cancer, a remedy for heart disease. A final end to war as a means of settling disputes. A binding agreement accepted by all nations to make our planet Earth a place where we can live in security and dignity. Others could be added.

But come back to marriage. Could making large numbers of marriages very much better be earthshaking? The answer is undoubtedly yes.

Mankind is at a critical point. Our magnificent technological achievements are backfiring. We have been rudely awakened from the dream that material abundance brings personal fulfillment. We are confronted with the ultimate problem of human relationships—how to get people to cooperate with each other to make life pleasant and fruitful for all.

And that, precisely, is what marriage is all about. It is the basic human relationship on which all the others ultimately depend.

Almost all of us started life in a family. During our impressionable early years, our world was a very small world, shaped by two people, a man and a woman. And the relationship between these two people set the pattern for all the other relationships that made up the rest of that small world's life. Far beyond any other influence in our entire lives, the way in which these two people·related to each other, the quality of life they achieved and demonstrated, made us what we are.

Multiply this again and again, and you have the authentic picture of human society. A man and a woman join to create a family. Together they try to provide the necessary conditions for their children to develop into mature adults, taking their place in the endless chain by which human culture is preserved and perpetuated. If they succeed, society benefits. If they fail, society suffers.

This is all so clear, so elementary, so obvious that we simply take it for granted. It is there all the time, we are looking at it all the time. And the startling result is that we end up with a blind spot and an inability to see the obvious. Yes, the obvious. It can be summed up in six simple, logical statements:

1. Our real human problem is not lack of knowledge, resources, or skill. We now have enough of these to enable us to achieve most of our goals.

2. Our problem is that we are failing to do the logical, necessary, and urgent things that need to be done, because of the failure of *people* to act cooperatively together for the common good.

3. People are failing to act cooperatively because too many of them habitually act in competition with one another, without consideration for one another's best interests, putting their own immediate personal gain before the common good.

4. *All* people do not act in this way. In every community there are some who show responsible and loving concern for the welfare of others. Communities with many people of this kind are good communities.

5. People with loving concern for the welfare of others

generally come from families in which they have learned this way of life from their earliest years.

6. Families in which the members learn to cooperate and to be lovingly concerned for one another's welfare are nearly always based on marriages in which husband and wife enjoy a warm and loving relationship.

The logic behind these propositions is surely self-evident.

All that is wrong is that we have not acted on that logic. We have allowed marriages to deteriorate as though they were unimportant. And now, we even talk of solving our problems by doing away with marriage altogether and replacing it with something else—something we are very vague about.

Isn't that rather like trying to repair a damaged building by pulling out the foundation stone? Wouldn't it be wise for us to think again? Particularly in view of the fact that we *can* have better marriages—if we really want them.

Forty Books for Further Reading

There is as yet little in the way of significant literature in the field of marriage enrichment. We have therefore put together here a somewhat miscellaneous list, including some of the older books along with the new, which may be of interest to readers wishing to explore further the ground covered in this volume. The list could have been expanded endlessly, so we limited it to forty titles. We have not attempted to give details about editions and prices, because these are constantly changing.

Bach, George R., and Wyden, Peter. *The Intimate Enemy*. William Morrow & Co., 1969. This book, which teaches the "art of marital fighting," aims at helping couples in conflict to achieve constructive communication.

Bernard, Jessie. *The Future of Marriage*. World Publishing Co., 1972. A searching investigation of modern marriage and some of its inadequacies, with some well-grounded predictions concerning its likely future development.

Blood, Robert O., and Wolfe, Donald M. *Husbands and Wives: The Dynamics of Married Living*. Free Press, 1960. The report of a comprehensive research project, highly respected by specialists in the field, and still often quoted by contemporary writers.

Bossard, James H. S., and Boll, Eleanor S. *Why Marriages Go Wrong*. Ronald Press, 1958. A critical appraisal of American marriage by two competent sociologists. Though dated, it is still worth reading.

Bovet, Theodor. *Love, Skill, and Mystery: A Handbook To Marriage*. Doubleday, 1958. A Swiss physician and lifelong student of marriage presents his concept of the partnership between husband and wife.

Bowman, Henry A. *Marriage for Moderns*. McGraw-Hill, 1960. One of the most popular college texts on marriage, written by one of the greatest teachers of marriage courses. Full of authoritative information.

Charney, Israel. *Marital Love and Hate*. Macmillan, 1972. A controversial discussion of the inevitable hostility that arises between marriage partners and the need to accept it as natural.

Cicero, Jim and June, and Fahs, Ivan and Joyce. *Conversations on Love and Sex in Marriage*. Word Books, 1972. An unusually frank exchange between two religious married couples about their sexual feelings and attitudes, tape-recorded and published verbatim.

Clinebell, Howard J. and Charlotte H. *The Intimate Marriage*. Harper & Row, 1970. Two marriage counselors, husband and wife, tell readers how their marriages can grow. One of the few books that focuses on marriage enrichment.

Denton, Wallace. *Family Problems and What To Do About Them*. Westminster Press, 1971. An excellent book about the stresses and strains which modern life imposes on marriage and family relationships.

Drakeford, John W. *Games Husbands and Wives Play*. Broadman Press, 1970. A book on marital interaction, with typical maneuvers engaged in by husbands and wives. Helps us to understand ourselves better.

Duvall, Evelyn M. *Family Development*. J. B. Lippincott, 1971. An authoritative work on modern families by a distinguished specialist in the field.

Fairchild, Roy W. *Christians in Families*. Covenant Life Curriculum Press, 1964. In a vast literature of rather sentimental books about Christian marriage and family life, this volume is in a class by itself.

Fisher, Esther O. *Help for Today's Troubled Marriages*. Hawthorne Books, 1968. A very sound and practical book about marriage counseling, free from needless technicalities.

Folkman, Jerome D., and Clatworthy, Nancy. *Marriage Has Many Faces*. Bobbs-Merrill, 1970. A marriage text for college students written by a Jewish Rabbi and a woman colleague. Accurate, up-to-date, and positive.

Gangsei, Lyle B. *Manual for Group Premarital Counseling*. Association Press, 1968. Selected material for a group of couples, arranged to stimulate discussion of various aspects of marriage.

Hamilton, Eleanor. *Partners in Love*. A. S. Barnes, 1968. In a very forthright but sensitive and understanding way, this book deals with the feeling aspect of the marriage relationship, including the sex relationship.

Havemann, Ernest. *Men, Women and Marriage*. Doubleday, 1962.

A professional writer puts together the significant facts about American marriage in more readable form than we find them in the bigger books.

Lederer, William J., and Jackson, Don D. *The Mirages of Marriage.* W. W. Norton, 1968. A provocative examination of marriage, stimulating to read and an excellent basis for discussion.

Levy, John, and Munro, Ruth. *The Happy Family.* Knopf, 1962. Revision of an old book which has become a classic, full of wisdom about husband-wife relationships.

Liswood, Rebecca. *First Aid for the Happy Marriage.* Trident Press, 1965. A physician with a warmly human and cheerful outlook writes about sex and marriage in very downright fashion with plenty of homespun wisdom.

Lobsenz, Norman M., and Blackburn, Clark W. *How to Stay Married.* Cowles, 1969. A professional writer teams up with the Executive Director of the Family Service Association of America to give us a practical guide to making marriage work.

Mace, David R. *Getting Ready for Marriage.* Abingdon Press, 1972. Written for the engaged couple, covering the procedures that would normally be used by an experienced marriage counselor in preparing them for marriage.

————. *Success in Marriage.* Abingdon Press, 1958. An examination of some of the hindrances to happy marriage and how to deal with them.

McGinnis, Tom. *Your First Year of Marriage.* Doubleday, 1967. An excellent and very practical guide, written by a distinguished marriage counselor, for newly marrieds and those preparing for marriage.

Magoun, F. Alexander. *Love and Marriage.* Harper & Row, 1956. An older book, written as a college text, full of wisdom and dry humor. One of our favorites.

Mudd, Emily H.; Mitchell, Howard E.; and Taubin, Sara B. *Success in Family Living.* Association Press, 1965. Based on a study of one hundred successful families, this book discusses what it takes to make a marriage work.

Otto, Herbert A. *More Joy in Your Marriage.* Cornerstone Library, 1971. A very practical book, full of ideas and suggestions for couples who want to develop the full potential of their marriage relationship.

————. *The Family in Search of a Future.* Appleton-Century-Crofts, 1970. This symposium covers effectively the many new life-styles that are being proposed today as substitutes for traditional marriage.

Peterson, James A. *Married Love in the Middle Years.* Association Press, 1968. An excellent book which deals with the neglected

171

subject of the middle-aged marriage, written by a highly qualified marriage counselor.

Plattner, Paul. *Conflict and Understanding in Marriage*. John Knox Press, 1970. A helpful little book dealing with the need to face and resolve conflict in every marriage.

Rogers, Carl. *Becoming Partners: Marriage and Its Alternatives*. Delacorte, 1972. A fascinating investigation based on interviews with couples who have tried out some of the new life-styles, with some helpful conclusions relevant to all marriages.

Samuel, Dorothy T. *Fun and Games in Marriage*. Word Books, 1973. A collection of short essays on marriage, sensitively written and handsomely printed. The author and her husband were among our early trainees and have led several marriage enrichment retreats.

Satir, Virginia. *Peoplemaking*. Science and Behavior Books, 1972. The author, a pioneer in family therapy, writes in her own vivid style about how family members grow through their interaction with each other.

Scanzoni, John. *Sexual Bargaining: Power Politics in the American Marriage*. Prentice-Hall, 1972. A penetrating analysis of what is happening to marriage today, with an unusually optimistic prognosis for its future.

Shedd, Charlie W. *Letters to Karen: On Keeping Love in Marriage*. Abingdon Press, 1965. A Methodist pastor, with a great gift for vivid and sensitive language, writes to his daughter, with penetrating insights, about her forthcoming marriage.

————. *Letters to Philip: On How to Treat a Woman*. Doubleday, 1968. A similar series of letters to his son.

Smith, Gerald W. *Me and You and Us*. Wyden, 1971. A practical handbook for couples seeking to improve their relationship, with forty-seven experiences they can share together. The author and his wife were participants in one of our early retreats.

Snow, John H. *On Pilgrimage: Marriage in the '70s*. Seabury Press, 1971. A chaplain at Princeton University defends marriage as the foundation of human society and calls for its revitalization as our primary task today.

Snyder, Ross. *Inscape*. Abingdon Press, 1968. Examines marriage as an intimate relationship through which both partners can develop their individual personalities.

Vincent, Clark E. *Sexual and Marital Health*. McGraw-Hill, 1973. Addressed primarily to physicians, but highly readable and full of stimulating ideas about how married couples can develop more effectively as companions, as sex partners, and as parents.